Your Multiple Souls

How They Direct Your Creativity, Genius, Complexity, and Moods

RUTH RENDELY

Your Multiple Souls
How They Direct Your Creativity, Genius, Complexity, and Moods
Ruth Rendely

Published by 1st World Publishing
P.O. Box 2211, Fairfield, Iowa 52556
tel: 641-209-5000 • fax: 866-440-5234
web: www.1stworldpublishing.com

First Edition

LCCN: 2015904105
Softcover ISBN: 978-1-4218-3724-6
Hardcover ISBN: 978-1-4218-3725-3
eBook ISBN: 978-1-4218-3726-0

The back cover quote from Neville Rowe (1939-1994) is taken from a 1993 unpublished book review he submitted to *The Journal of Regression Therapy* after reading Ruth's 17-page booklet *Multiple Souls* (Sydney: 1992). Neville was a world leader of Past-Life Regression Therapy.

These two men will always have a place in my heart:

Neville Rowe (1939-1994),
a New Zealand dolphin channel,
and past-life regression therapist

Reverend Joseph Martinez (1941-1995),
a Filipino-American psychic surgeon,
former Catholic monk, who founded a Spiritual Healing
Center in San Francisco in the 1980s

ALSO BY RUTH RENDELY

Seraphim Blueprint

Multiple Souls

Acknowledgements

This book was divinely inspired by the continual personal training from my main spirit guide, Babaji, of the Yogananda tradition. For at least eighteen years this wonderful avatar stayed at my side as he introduced me to new concepts and people who would further my understanding that human souls can share bodies, something barely mentioned in historical and literary sources.

In the two decades it has taken me to finish this project, I have had quite a few readers and several editors. I wish to thank my first editor, Amanita Rosenbush, for her healthy intellectual skepticism regarding the main thesis of the book, which challenged me to think and write more clearly for people who might be unconvinced by the ideas presented herein. The opinions and editing of Susan Batho, Australian rabbit show enthusiast, helped me to see that the end was in sight. I am especially grateful to my treasured friend Angela Mailander, who yet again agreed to take on the detailed editing, after navigating me through my first book as well. She has the distinction of making important conceptual additions to the final work. Then, for a final edit I wish to thank my old friend John Jeffrey Kennedy for his wonderful polishing skills. Also, throughout the past twenty years, an accomplished writer on spiritual matters—Andrew Ramer—author of *Ask Your Angels*, cheered me on. And in the last stages of writing, my husband Ron has been my rock, sharing my spiritual values, intellectually sparring with me to keep me on my toes, and at the same time selflessly taking care of the practical chores on our property, while I spent time communing with the gods.

Preface

Since 1989, when I first started formulating my multiple-soul theory, I have certainly encountered detractors all along the way. Among these critics were fellow intuitives with years of accumulated consulting experience. Occasionally, of course, one would take my theory seriously, especially after reading my 17-page published precursor to this book called *Multiple Souls* (c.1992, Sydney). However, when I moved to Berkeley, California, in 1994, I met with firm opposition from a new spiritual mentor, one who had a strong academic background and was well-read in religious studies. He categorically informed me that there was no record of such a soul theory in any major mystical tradition, not in the Kabbalah, or in any other ancient source, and that I was wasting my time exploring this notion regarding the nature of the soul. He felt that I had been investigating what was essentially a dead end, and that I needed to go back to square one and start over. His guides did inform him, however, that it was my soul's purpose to explore soul phenomena. He counseled me that I would do better pursuing something along the lines of the soul's complexity—by considering it analogous to the facets of a cut diamond. I liked his analogy, although it did not hold my attention for very long. Still, I so respected his opinion at the time that I sincerely tried to rethink my theory. This mentor, who was a former university professor and on a first-name basis with many angels and spirit guides, in effect sidetracked me from working on the present book for a year and a half, while I processed the significance of his critical assessment.

In the meantime, however, I continued to find my original ideas far too compelling to turn back—most of all due to their continual confirmation in my work with clients. Besides, before this man proffered his adverse view, I had met two other soul workers whom I greatly esteemed and who lent support to my theory: Neville Rowe, a New Zealand past-life regression therapist and dolphin channeler, and Reverend Joseph Martinez, founder of the San Francisco Spiritual Healing Center, both spiritual teachers with strong followings.

Neville was initially skeptical of my multiple-soul hypothesis, but came around to both appreciate and encourage the idea. Rev. Martinez, when he first heard me mention the notion, said he was indeed aware of "fused souls" and was thus aligned with my thinking. Unfortunately, both men, who could have been great collaborators in the years following, suddenly died. Neville died within about a year and a half of our first acquaintance, and Joseph, about a month and a half after we met. In their final days, and hours, they continued to sustain my work, but since they departed so quickly, I found myself at a bit of a loss without their help.

Yet, even without any intellectual underpinnings, I continued to use the model within a tentative, wait-and-see framework. I had stopped writing this book, yes, but I continued to apply the multiple-soul theory to my work with those among my clients who, I felt, needed that kind of insight. Experiencing ongoing success with such applications, I became more confident in openly discussing the concept. By April of 1994, I was invited to speak about my work at the San Francisco Whole Life Expo. The room was filled with over one hundred attendees, who seemed greatly receptive to this new idea about the soul.

Nevertheless, before I could refine the theory, I still sought historical confirmation. I was stunned around this time when I consulted the *Encyclopedia Britannica*, of all things, and found an exact listing entitled: "Multiple Souls". In it I discovered that the few cultures in which such a concept existed were not using it in the same way I was. Manchurian tradition, for example, included the idea that different aspects of the soul ruled different parts of the body. In ancient Egypt, for our word 'soul' the language contained nine words, each with slight gradations of meaning. In all such cases, however, I found that the concept was either marginal to the culture or obscured within arcane shamanic doctrine.

The real breakthrough came, finally, because of my proximity to the Graduate Theological Union, with its close ties to the University of California, Berkeley. One day I saw in a local newspaper a reference to Daniel C. Matt, Professor of Jewish Mysticism on that school's faculty, and I immediately contacted his office for an appointment. I brought my 17-page booklet with me. When I arrived he allowed me to record our hour-long conversation. Initially I described how I came to develop this theory, and I also mentioned the strong opposition from my mentor, who held that such ideas didn't exist in ancient texts and that they were even warned against. I then asked Professor Matt for his opinion on the matter.

He replied: "[In the Kabbalah] There is a mention of what's called *gilgul*, transmigration. But within *gilgul* it's called *ibbur*, which is another soul coming into a body that already has a soul." Continuing, he said:

"The first thing I would say is that you have got to find out anything you can about *ibbur*, as certainly that is the closest thing in Kabbalah to what you are talking about... The idea of multiple souls would be unusual, but it is certainly not unheard of in Kabbalah."

Then he gave me the titles of several reference books to

confirm what he was saying. I was ecstatic. Since that meeting twenty years ago, Professor Matt has continued to build on his reputation as one of the foremost scholars on Kabbalah and has recently completed eight volumes of a 12-volume English translation from the original Aramaic of the *Zohar*, the central text of Kabbalah.

After a year and a half of seriously doubting my intuition regarding my theory, I felt vindicated and took a renewed interest in writing the present book.

It appears that in the thirteenth century the early Jewish Kabbalists began serious discussions of reincarnation theories. The Hebrew word for reincarnation is *gilgul*, which means 'rolling over'. Gershom Scholem (1897-1982), the foremost twentieth-century historian of Kabbalah, after describing the major developments in thirteenth-century Kabbalistic theory, indicated how a new aspect of reincarnation theory emerged at that time:

"Not all migrating souls enter the new body at the moment of conception or of birth; sometimes, at special moments during the course of his life, a person receives a second soul that is, so to speak, impregnated within his own soul. This additional soul is not linked to his psychophysical organism from birth nor does it partake in its development, but can accompany him until his death or may leave him earlier. According to the Zohar, the souls of certain pious figures in the Bible were impregnated with the deceased souls of other righteous men from the past at decisive moments in their lives. .... at a particular moment, and for the performance of a particular deed (such as Boaz's marriage to Ruth, who had been impoverished by the loss of her first husband in war), a soul returns and descends (even from Paradise!) in order to strengthen and encourage another soul in the performance of a given act.

Henceforth, beginning around 1300, the term '*ibbur*' [impregnation] is used to designate the process taking place in a living body, as distinct from *gilgul*, which signifies the incarnation of a soul in a body from the moment of conception."[1]

With such validation from ancient Judaism, I felt more confident that I was on the right path in my discovery that many of my clients did, in fact, have multiple souls, and I have continued over the past two decades in furthering and deepening my ideas regarding this theory.

Now, subsequent to many more successful soul interventions with clients, I realize that numerous problems in society are misdiagnosed—from depression to murder—all because multiple-soul theory is unknown. My hope in writing this book is that this state of affairs will change. I feel that humanity is ready to recognize this fuller possibility, and that we can take our mutual evolution up to the next level.

Ruth Rendely
Blue Ridge Mountains
Winter 2015

---

[1] "Gilgul: The Transmigration of Souls," *On the Mystical Shape of the Godhead: Basic Concepts in the Kabbalah,* by Gershom Scholem (New York: Schocken Books, English copyright 1991), p. 222.

Chapter 1

The Dilemma

"I'm sorry to bother you, Ruth, but it's an emergency."
It was the summer of 1990, around mid-December,
when I first heard about Richa Varma. I had been living in
Sydney, Australia, only a few months when Dr. Rajiv Nayar,
a new friend, woke me with an early morning call.

"A friend's daughter is in serious trouble," he went on.
"Three weeks ago, my friend left his baby girl with relatives
while he and his wife went to New Zealand. Then they had
to cut their vacation short because their daughter was experiencing severe convulsions and had to be hospitalized."

"Had she been diagnosed with any pre-existing condition?"

"No, nothing. But now she has been in hospital for three
weeks, and the strongest anti-convulsive drugs don't seem to
be working. Even though my friend is also a doctor, he has
little hope. He is so anxious and feels that there is nothing left
to do for his little girl. But the reason I am calling you is that
I have a suspicion that this may not be a medical problem."

As I listened to Rajiv my mind was already racing ahead to
other possibilities, but I said,

"What do you mean?"

"It may be a spiritual problem."

Rajiv had come to me several times for counseling. He
had hoped that I could help resolve his conflicted feelings

between the material world of being a medical doctor and the spiritual world of Indian mysticism. Growing up in India, he had experienced profound trance states, but now he had the responsibilities of being a family man. He had yet to integrate these two paths.

"What is the little girl's name?"

"Her name is Richa Varma."

He then supplied me with the names of the parents. I said I would call him back when I had discussed Richa's situation with someone I had in mind.

When I looked at the energy of the little girl, I found she had a lost soul that was attacking her on a psychic plane. The term "lost soul" refers to a deceased human being who resists leaving their material life behind, usually because they have failed to achieve closure in the dramas of their recent incarnation. In Richa's case, I felt the lost soul might be a recently deceased female relative, possibly her grandmother, who was covetous of the little girl's new earthly life.

I then called a young woman I had met the previous August. Originally from Scotland, Sharon had spoken of having beautiful clairvoyant visions as a child. She and I felt a strong past-life connection and had bonded deeply from our first chance meeting in a Sydney café. Under my tutelage, she was quickly restoring psychic and spiritual abilities she had lost through unsound lifestyle choices. Speaking almost daily, we respected each other's perceptions concerning difficult cases such as this one.

That morning, Sharon confirmed my "lost soul" diagnosis of Richa's condition and immediately proceeded to remove the soul (another ability she had). She would first detect the entity attached to the child's body and then ask spirit guides to detach the lost soul and send it to the Light.

I quickly redialed Rajiv's number. I told him that a recently deceased, elderly relative, envious of the baby girl, had been attacking her. Now that Sharon had assisted in removing the entity, we expected the girl's convulsions to cease.

I then asked Rajiv to be a go-between for me with Richa's father, mentioning that I would like to talk with him if he felt comfortable with my calling. I later heard from Rajiv that the father had agreed. That afternoon I called his office.

I inquired if there had been any change in his daughter's convulsions. He responded that there had been a fluctuation in the pattern, but it was too soon to tell whether this was really an improvement. I then offered my services as a healer, hoping that I could do some hands-on healing on Richa in the hospital. He declined my offer, but agreed to consider it for the future.

That was a Thursday. The following Saturday evening a close friend, who had just founded a New Age center in Sydney, invited Sharon and me to a housewarming party. I had also invited Dr. Nayar to meet my friends. He arrived with his wife and young son.

After initial pleasantries, Dr. Nayar drew me aside and said, "Richa's convulsions haven't stopped. We no longer want you to work on the case. We now plan to call upon the services of a Brahmin priest."

I relayed this to Sharon in private, and we gave each other a knowing look. With her pendulum as usual in her right hand, she started swinging it to determine what was really occurring in Richa's case.

By the following morning, Sharon had discovered a second cause for Richa's ailment. She said, "The key is in her name— Ri Cha. One soul calls herself 'Ri'; the other soul calls herself 'Cha'. The two souls are fighting for control of her body. They have been fused together for several lifetimes. Cha had been dominant in the last lifetime and is trying to continue that dominance into the current life. Ri is putting up a fight."

"So what did you do about this?" I asked.

"Well, I explained to the two souls that neither would succeed if the body died, and that one of them should agree to leave. After much coaxing, Cha, the dominant soul, agreed to go, once I said that whichever soul remained was going to have a difficult life."

Sharon and I had been discussing and refining our perception of multiple souls ever since her birthday the previous August. As a birthday gift, I had given her a Soul Reading, and as part of the reading, I had told her that some of those closest to her had more than one soul. She had been quick to accept this novel idea, and soon she was adding new elements to this knowledge as she talked with her own spirit guides.

As I listened to Sharon explain the battle between Richa's two souls, I felt she had discovered the root cause of the malady. We both agreed that there most likely had been a jealous lost soul involved, but that was a superficial irritant compared to the outright struggle between two souls. We then concluded there was no reason to call anyone with this news since we were not supposed to be working on Richa. We went about our business as usual.

The following Wednesday Dr. Nayar called me. "Her convulsions have ceased. She is out of danger. The father and I want to thank you and Sharon from the bottom of our hearts."

"Why are you thanking us?" I asked.

"Because we hadn't yet called the priest."

Only then did I tell him about Sharon's discovery of the two souls fighting over Richa's body, and how Sharon had coaxed one of them to leave. Rajiv had heard me discuss multiple souls before. He now seemed to accept this explanation as it applied to Richa.

Elated with the outcome in Richa's case, I immediately phoned Sharon to share the good news. We decided to celebrate that afternoon at a nearby café. Once there, we

discussed how the "Richa Story" might be a tentative validation of the idea of multiple souls.

Before Richa's case, we had both assumed that having more
than one soul was a benign situation, resulting in the person
being more talented than a one-souled individual, drawing
on the abilities of the different souls. It seemed that the only
drawbacks involved moodiness and possibly indecision. Now
we knew that there could be other, gloomier scenarios.

I asked Sharon whether we should go public.

"Absolutely not! I want no publicity about this. We need
to proceed quietly."

"But what if something like this were to happen again?" I
protested.

"They are not to contact me directly, but they can go
through you. I don't even want them to know my name."

Sharon and I thus cautiously agreed to formalize our
teamwork to help solve new cases. We were both excited
and a bit daunted by this prospect. Until the Richa case, the
multiple-soul idea had been tentative, without any known
applications. Most of my multiple-souled acquaintances were
perfectly normal, albeit complex individuals.

On that day in 1990, however, when Dr. Nayar called to
thank us, Sharon and I celebrated. We felt, rightly or wrongly,
that we had for the first time successfully dealt with a problem
resulting from multiple souls. Although we did not know all
the facts about Richa, and to this day have not met her, it was
the experience we gained in healing her that later resulted in
many more cases having positive outcomes.

Now, over a thousand interventions later, the story of
Richa has come to have a mythic quality for me. Her case
marked a turning point in my life.

Chapter 2

The Nature of the Soul

Man is a soul, and he has a body.
> —Paramahansa Yogananda

Having just read my account of what occurred in 1990, you might wonder why it has taken me twenty-five years to write about it. I often sat in front of my computer attempting to convey this information, but even merely contemplating putting these ideas out into the public domain gave me pause when I realized the implications. If the public took the concept of multiple souls seriously, the impact on psychology, criminology, education, and religion would be part of a great paradigm shift. Once people realize that some of us are multi-souled, while others are single-souled, could there be a basis for a new type of discrimination, and/or a new form of political correctness? Taking this idea to heart does have the potential for being life-changing.

In the early 1990's, I thought *surely* I am not alone in being the custodian of this novel theory. Surely, I reasoned, some other clairvoyant would have simultaneously plucked this idea from the ether and any day now would write about multiple souls. But having waited in vain for twenty years, I now know that it is my soul's purpose to publish these findings. I also now have more confidence in answering relevant questions, based upon two decades of professional service and personal experience.

While writing this type of book might bring many new clients to an author, I cannot foresee how I could take on any additional work, due to other commitments. In a way, it is unfortunate that souls cannot be cloned, or I would duplicate myself many times over to help people who have problems at the soul level. Since it is nearly impossible for me to train others in the skills I was either gifted with or have acquired doing this work, it will take someone with very special spiritual abilities to even consider working in this way.

The presentation of this material is to help you know yourself, as well as others close to you, with the aid of the descriptions and examples in the book. It is also written to help interested academics and spiritual seekers form a new baseline understanding of the true nature of the soul, in order to create a fresh avenue for exploring the depths of our collective experience.

I am also writing this to acquaint you with a hidden, currently neglected aspect of the human condition. Let us now place this novel theory into an historical and cultural context.

In the more than 6,000 years of recorded history, there has been little agreement about the nature of the soul. In attempting to define the soul, most people who have tried to do so fall on a continuum between materialism and spiritualism. Historically, materialists have conflated the soul with matter. Absolute materialists do not believe the soul exists. Spiritualists sometimes fuse the soul with God, thus eliminating the soul as a separate entity.

The ancient Greeks initiated this confusion about the nature of the soul when Plato, Socrates, and Pythagoras agreed that the soul (*psyche*) was immortal and distinct from the body.

Aristotle, however, placed the soul firmly in the body, omitting the idea that the soul was immortal. So the materialism of Aristotle was in direct opposition to the spiritual ideas of the Platonists. While the latter generally agreed upon the immortality of the soul, they nevertheless spent much of their time discussing its location in the body.

Christianity adopted the Platonic mind-body dualism with its emphasis on an immortal soul, but less on principle and more on a practical need to console adherents who were concerned about survival after death. The Church limited the discussion of the nature of the "soul" during the many centuries of its supremacy in Europe.

Unlike the Western world, which became ever more materialist in outlook, the Eastern world, represented here by the Hindu tradition, tended to fall into the spiritual, non-dualist camp. For instance, in the Bhagavad-Gita, (Chapter 2, Verse 18) we see some evidence of this:

> *These bodies are known to have an end; the dweller in the body is eternal, imperishable, infinite.*

And referring to the soul as "he"[1] in Verse 20:

> *He is never born, nor does he ever die; nor once having been, does he cease to be. Unborn, eternal, everlasting, ancient, he is not slain when the body is slain.*

This Vedic concept breaks the ties with materiality via a negative path. The soul is *not* the body, *not* the mind, *not* the ego, *not* the heart. By following this path, all becomes the One, eternal Brahman, or Godhead. Godhead, in turn, creates the universe in terms of what is called *Veda Lila*, the divine play of the Absolute. According to this idea, multiple souls make infinite diversity within Unity possible.

> **Multiple souls make infinite diversity within Unity possible.**

---

[1] This is probably the result of grammatical gender in Sanskrit, rather than sexism.

Coming back to our Western roots, since the 1600's, with the ascendancy of scientific materialism and its replacement of the Church at the center of our lives, the subject of "soul" has been relegated to a dusty back closet. Although the modern world inherited the term "soul" from antiquity, when the ancients universally believed in some form of it, modern secular humanists have denied its very existence. Confining it to the world of religion, they have tried to taint and sink it, along with all religious belief. Since universities are filled with secular humanists and materialists, they are not interested in researching a subject they do not believe corresponds to any kind of reality, except as a curious relic related to ancient philosophy and history. Modern religious institutions are also averse to studying the subject of the soul because any novelties discovered might undermine their followers' beliefs and their own authority. Thus, at present, research into the concept and the reality of the soul is practically nonexistent.

Even now, this continued inattention prevents the development of the 'science of soul'. Serious researchers would first have to waste time in simply establishing the very *existence* of the soul.

However, things are beginning to change. Many recent thinkers have seen the chink in the armor of physics because of Werner Heisenberg's famed Uncertainty Principle, in which it appears that the "observer"—that utterly subjective aspect— is central to the *outcome* of experiments of advanced particle physics. Given this opportunity, some scientists and spiritualists are hurrying to create new theories bridging the chasm that exists between them and their institutions. The majority of the members of both camps, however, still prefer an adversarial model. While science is regrouping its forces, those that have been thinking about the subject of the soul have come forth to take a stand—myself included.

I see the soul as an energetic envelope, separate from the

body, and as a discretely diluted version of God—something like a homeopathic elixir, where the original substance can no longer be found in the potion, but something of God's essence is still there. From my perception, if the soul could be visible, it would be larger than the body. This is the view that has evolved for me through many years of study and experience, and, as you will see in my story, there were stages in my career when this had not yet become clear.

Energy, however, implies materiality, and thus I take a middle position between those who reduce the soul to an epiphenomenon of material function and those who inflate the soul to God. This energy envelope that I am proposing surrounds the body like a cloud or mist, which at some points is attached to the body—indicative of more complete absorption in those locations. I believe that Aristotelian materialists are partly correct when they try to place the soul inside of the body. The soul is attached to part of the body, but *which part* may vary from person to person.

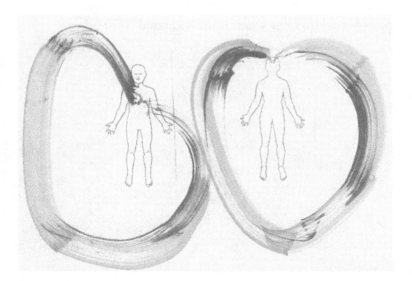

This localized connection between body and soul may explain why particular attributes of an individual, i.e., "a brilliant mind" or "a beautiful heart", may actually have their foundation in soul energy highlighting these particular areas— the soul may be more infused or "corded" in these locations.

Furthermore, the soul likely has an interdimensional and timeless nature that is not restricted by our planetary clock, or even by the third dimension. Flashes of precognition and fears lingering from distant eons or other intergalactic locales are no doubt impinging upon our subconscious at all times. I have in recent years become aware of other dimensional realities because of recurring dreams that seem very real, with an ongoing internal development that bespeaks of an alternate life occurring simultaneously with this one.

Thus, to sum up, 'the soul' could be defined as a genderless entity with a personal history going back to its birth at a particular point in space and time. The soul has its own qualities, karma, memory, and maturation process. These developments span thousands and possibly millions of years from the primordial moment when it individuated from Source.

Chapter 3

Preparation

The soul is com-plicated, a word whose literal meaning is 'woven together'.

—Thomas Moore

In looking back over my life, I have wondered what factors contributed to my multiple-soul discovery. I might never know conclusively, but I suspect that I possess an unusual mixture of openness to new information, along with a deep appreciation of world history, religion, and cultural patterns from many lands and past ages. As I matured, I became increasingly aware of the spiritual dimension and my own psychic gifts. These gifts have also required that I be centered enough to know whether I am being deceived by nonphysical beings, or am instead being truly led down a path towards new knowledge about the human condition.

My openness to new information and new ways of looking at the world may have been the result of being part of a small minority in the fabric of American society, as I am a granddaughter of poor Jewish immigrants who arrived in New York at the beginning of the twentieth century, and I am thus a third-generation American. In my case, this heritage helped make me sensitive, curious, bookish, and shy. When at age twelve I read the *Diary of Ann Frank*, I identified with her so completely that I wondered if I had her reincarnated soul. I am not even sure that at that time I knew much about the meaning of reincarnation, though I do remember being slightly disappointed when I discovered that she died a year after I was born.

I grew up to love school, reading, studying, and teaching history. I always had a sense of destiny, that I was fated to make a unique contribution to society. I enjoyed being different and felt little need to conform to either my own heritage or to that of the wider American culture. When I was two years old, the first-born, my mother spoke to me as an adult. When she told me a year later about the German concentration camps, I understood what she meant, and knew that it was important to prevent such insanity from ever happening again. I didn't resent her for taking away my childhood innocence, but instead I let that revelation form me in ways that distinguished me from other children.

In my teens and twenties, I excelled at many things, but like many people, I lacked clarity about my life purpose. Because of this confusion, and with the assistance of scholarships that supported my lifestyle, I became a perennial student. Any nonacademic work I undertook before the age of forty-five was casual and impermanent.

My alienation, though, resulted in two life-changing experiences that opened me up to new vistas. One was a deep imbibing of Japanese language and culture, and the other was the adoption of an Eastern meditation practice.

During my sophomore year at George Washington University (on a full-tuition scholarship), a fellow student, who happened to be from an elite Japanese political family, started to take a romantic interest in me. His exoticness, handsomeness, intelligence, and charisma resulted in my falling in love with him. It was a kind of forbidden love on both of our parts—his, because he was being groomed to be prime minister of Japan, and mine because my parents expected me to date only Jewish men.

Because of my parents, I told Takashi that I could only see him midweek, so as to not arouse their suspicion. Ours was a clandestine relationship through the spring of 1963. But as we became emotionally closer, Takashi insisted on meeting my parents. By this time, my younger sister had told my mother that I was in love with a Japanese student who had mysteriously disappeared from the university. That part was true, as Takashi suddenly dropped out of his classes, and even the university authorities were told only that he had to go back to Japan for a family emergency. Because of my scholarship, I couldn't afford to let this romance affect my grade point average, so I threw myself into my studies as I prepared for finals week at the end of the spring semester.

As I sat on the grass near the Student Union studying for exams, one of our mutual friends came out of the Union to say that Takashi had suddenly reappeared and wanted to see me. Peeved that he hadn't told me his reason for leaving school nor written to me from Japan, I told this friend that I didn't have time for him, even though my heart was pounding with joy. Takashi then came out to me, and tried to explain the reason he had left so precipitously.

Still, the cultural differences between us were enormous, and my parents were happy that I was scheduled to make a long-anticipated summer trip to stay on an Israeli kibbutz. My ticket was paid for with babysitting money I had earned during my teenage years, and I was locked into a three-month stay in Israel about three weeks hence.

Takashi did meet my parents, however, and I will never forget how low he bowed to my father as my dad opened our front door. This bow totally disarmed my father, who immediately took a liking to him. A few years later, within days of my first trip to Japan, Takashi and I briefly became engaged

when he was 25 and I was 23. But it was years before such international marriages were approved in his culture, so he broke
it off, knowing that an inter-racial marriage would prevent his
political aspirations, something I had realized as soon as I heard
about his background in the first weeks of our relationship.

This romance consumed most of my early twenties and
resulted in my life-long interest in Japanese culture. In 1966,
again through scholarships, I was offered the opportunity to
live in Kyoto, Japan, for a year, with the sole purpose of learning
the language. Japan of that era was much less Westernized
than it is now. Hardly anybody spoke English, so I managed
to learn to speak rudimentary Japanese in about six months'
time. Meanwhile, almost everything about the Japanese way
of life was opposite, or at least different, from American life-
styles. It was a first-hand experience of how much language
and culture can influence one's mental processes and worldview. Years later, I realized that I might have learned to speak
Japanese so quickly because I had probably had past lives in
Japan—so possibly I was simply reviving old skills.

My past-life attachment to Japan must have been quite
deep, because I was not taken in by the charms of Hawaii
when I returned there after a year in Japan. I felt as if I was
just marking time before my return to Japan. As I had hoped,
I was selected by the American government to be a bilingual
guide for the American Pavilion at Osaka's International Expo
in 1970.

Although being a guide in the Pavilion appeared to be
glamorous, it was the most stressful job of my life. In those
years, the concept of stress building in the body was little understood, but watching thousands of people passing in front
of me every hour that I stood in the Pavilion was indeed a
stressful experience, especially when it went on for six months,
and when those visiting the Pavilion had waited four hours
in line in the sweltering heat before coming inside. My love

affair with all things Japanese was being tested.

Nevertheless, all the strain of that job helped me to have another life-changing experience, which reduced those high stress levels. In 1972, when I was living and teaching high school history in Honolulu, Hawaii, my younger sister, Marsha, convinced me to start meditating according to the Transcendental Meditation program as taught by Maharishi Mahesh Yogi. I was the last one in my family to learn to meditate. Marsha had become a teacher of Transcendental Meditation under the tutelage of Maharishi. After she taught my parents to meditate, she persuaded me to learn.

At the time I told myself meditation was only for releasing stress, as I was reluctant to admit that I needed help, and I was resistant to anything quasi-religious. I was proud of my advanced history degree, my ability to speak Japanese, and my stint in the U.S. Foreign Service. It was 1972, and I felt foolish learning anything related to religion, especially this Indian hippie meditation, which I saw as a fringe phenomenon.

As the benefits of meditating began to accrue, however, my skepticism was challenged. After a year of meditating, I recognized that my stress levels were dropping—this despite my increasing dissatisfaction with my teaching job. Thus, in a case of sibling reversal, I turned to my younger sister for guidance in setting a new life course. She suggested that if I needed a new direction, I might want to take her job as Director of Admissions at Maharishi International University in Santa Barbara, California, since she was planning to attend a short teacher-training course in Europe with Maharishi Mahesh Yogi. By that time, I was living and working in Northern California, so it was easy for me to move to the Santa Barbara campus in Southern California.

The position paid room, board, and a $75 monthly stipend. The main reason others were interested in working for these wages was to earn course credits toward becoming a meditation instructor. At the time, I felt such a course was an opportunity for me to 'get my head together' and plan my next 'real' life situation. If I worked long enough in Santa Barbara, I would earn the six-month meditation teacher-training course to be held at a Swiss resort. At the very least, this opportunity promised to be a great European vacation.

With each passing week at the Santa Barbara meditation facility, my skepticism was turning into admiration for all the changes I was witnessing in myself and others. The new students that I was admitting to the school were mellowing before my eyes, thus challenging my preconceived notions about this meditation movement. When I had been working there six months, events transpired in such a way that I was able to go to Europe to attend the first three months of teacher-training in the Italian Alps. Within a few weeks of my arrival in Livigno, Italy, our course was scheduled to meet Maharishi in circumstances that would make it very clear to me that he had gifts beyond anything I had previously known to exist on this planet. In that three-month course, I changed from being an exceedingly pessimistic person, to one who became exceptionally optimistic. I also lost about 15 pounds in the process, which was an unforeseen benefit and counterintuitive to sitting twelve hours a day, either with my eyes closed or watching videos of Maharishi.

For the next three years I felt everything I did and touched was supported by unseen beneficial energy or freaky good luck. Maharishi called this phenomenon "support of nature". The TM movement meanwhile bought a bankrupt college in Fairfield, Iowa. After teacher-training, I went back to working full-time for the TM movement and lived in that cocoon for another year. Even when I moved away, it was only sixty miles away, to Iowa City, where I began my doctoral work in American intellectual history at the University of Iowa—again on a full-tuition scholarship for the following four years.

Thus, I had experienced two major life-changing influences that convinced me beyond any doubt that the human mind was malleable and could create changes in the real world. I now knew from experience that anything was possible, and I was alert to discovering the unusual, knowing that as an American teacher of Transcendental Meditation who spoke fluent Japanese, I was somewhat unique. Still, I was following in the footsteps of others, not creating something new.

My mother's unexpected death in 1987 triggered the most soul-searching I had done in my life. I had wanted to complete my doctorate, both because of the ten years invested, but also to please her. Later, I would come to realize that her death not only freed me from her expectations concerning my academic achievements, but also empowered me with her passion for service.

In the last three weeks of her life, as she was dying of melanoma and I was ministering to her needs, I had been impressed with the alternative healing methods of the four psychic healers I had asked to work on my mother's case—two in Japan (where I was currently living) and two in America. Having drafted the help of these psychic healers, I gained a special respect for their abilities. Although the healers hadn't prolonged her life, they did reduce her suffering. My mother received no pain medication, nor did she ask for any, and her death seemed remarkably peaceful.

During the several weeks of caring for her, I had many opportunities to discuss her condition with the healers. One of them was reluctant to take the case, but yielded when she psychically discovered the worthiness of the candidate. She exclaimed: "Your mother has such a big heart!" These conversations engendered a curious thought: Wouldn't it be wonderful to become a psychic healer? So many people could be helped this way, without drugs and their horrendous side effects. At the time though, my belief system, which assumed that one had to be born with such abilities, prevented me from thinking about this too much. My own psychic experiences were rather limited: just to an occasional episode, such as a serendipitous meeting or a premonition in a dream, something many people occasionally experience. In short, when I compared my capabilities with my close circle of friends, all of whom were TM teachers, nothing I experienced came close to their flashy, visionary accounts of seeing angels, fairies, and their own past lives.

It was because of my profound mid-life crisis, however—involving my mother's death, a breakup with a boyfriend, and the University of Iowa's history department's rejection of my doctoral dissertation—that I was open enough to let in new ways of looking at the psychic suffering of others.

Regarding the rejection of my doctoral thesis, I was not savvy enough in the ways of academia to understand the politics of my situation at the University of Iowa, one hour's drive from the new campus of Maharishi International University (MIU). MIU was considered a cult school by the faculty of the state university. And the subject of my doctoral thesis, which was titled *A Foundation of Ecstasy: The American Shaker Experience*, had allowed me to go deeply into a culture that reminded me of the Transcendental Meditation movement. Similar to the TM movement, Shakers had utopian communal ideas based upon mystical experiences. Since I had recently spent three years in the bosom of the Transcendental Meditation community on the campus in Fairfield, Iowa, I was quite sympathetic to the Shaker movement, which had occurred 100 years earlier. The problem for my dissertation committee, first of all, was that I couldn't find anything to disprove my thesis that the Shakers' incredible creative and inventive abilities were based upon their ecstatic, mystical practices. And then, secondly, anything outside of the materialist Western worldview was not allowed. So much for academic freedom.

With the shattering of my future academic career, I had to let go of my self-image as an intellectual—someone whose world-view was based on the intellect—very left-brain, clinical, distant, leaving little room for compassion. That fateful year, 1987, I began to realize that I lacked sympathy for the misery of others, often blaming victims for their sorry state. Slowly, at that time, I saw that when people asked me for help, I was, in fact, being offered a choice to become more compassionate. In those days, as I experienced the deep pain others often experience, I developed a degree of sympathy for their plight. When I acted to help them in some small way, I temporarily forgot my own pain. As I began to notice this, it became clear to me that this was the only lifeline I was being given. I grabbed it.

The psychic pain I had been experiencing was unending, and I felt like I was learning a new inner landscape, with lots of time to study the details and nuances. Although I had felt an unexplained loneliness and sadness for much of my life, I had likewise felt incapable of helping others with their own pain. When friends sought my counsel, I would mostly suggest logical, left-brain steps of action. Little did I understand how one might relieve one's own pain by helping others. It takes almost a leap of faith to make the transition from focusing on one's own pain, and right in the *midst* of that pain, instead offer help to others. The rational approach would be to first heal yourself before attempting to heal others, but the counterintuitive approach—of throwing oneself into the process of healing others—often results in one's own healing as well. Establishing a habit of helping others first, and seeing the fruit of that help, finally blessed me with true happiness, and with personal health as a by-product.

Chapter 4

An Indian Saint Appears

Read

Before I had realized that helping others might help me to recover from my deep depression, I desperately tried different methods to heal myself. In early May, 1987, I remembered that I had a copy of *The Autobiography of a Yogi* by Paramahansa Yogananda, and I decided that the book's uplifting messages might help me heal.

Yogananda's adventures were so extraordinary and miraculous that one could hardly imagine experiencing them in a human body. Yogananda wrote about living swamis who were seen in two places at once, saints who levitated, and even one saint who never slept. In each case, Yogananda's description of these saints was so compelling that his account overcame my natural skepticism. Also, because of my meditation teacher-training, I trusted that an enlightened guru would be truthful to his followers and wouldn't publish fabricated stories as part of his personal life experience.

I knew that our beliefs could define what we are able to see. Therefore, it is much more difficult for us to trust what someone else says has occurred distantly in time or space. For instance, Catholicism has many adherents in the world, but how many of them would believe St. Teresa of Avila, a sixteenth-century Catholic nun, who wrote in her autobiography about her multiple experiences of levitation? As the founding abbess of a new order of nuns, she instructed her assistants to hold her down if she started to lift up in the middle of Sunday services, so as not to shock the visiting townswomen.

> She instructed her assistant to hold her down if she started to lift up....

In any case, I chose to believe Yogananda's experiences, and I was soon greatly rewarded. Paramahansa Yogananda (1893-1952) was a disciple of Shri Yukteswar (1855-1936), who in turn was a disciple of Lahiri Mahasaya (1828-1895). Before he became a yogi, Lahiri had been a postal worker stationed in the high Himalayas. Then, in 1861, there appeared before him an illuminated being, who seemed to be about 25 years old and who gave spiritual instruction to Lahiri. These teachings were later relayed to his followers, some of whom several decades later also interacted with the ever-youthful man they referred to as *Babaji*.

The birth and origins of Babaji were unknown, but it was thought that he had possibly been alive in the same body since about 200 AD. Yogananda's spiritual lineage referred to him as a *mahavatar*, or **"great avatar"**. Before the Internet and a subsequent movie corrupted this Sanskrit word, *avatar* referred to "a being that is a direct manifestation of God". Satyananda, a disciple of Yogananda's, said the following about a *mahavatar*.

> *"Throughout human evolution we're evolving physically, but we're also evolving spiritually. And the pinnacle of spiritual evolution is a cosmic consciousness that unites our awareness with all three worlds [physical, causal, astral], and beyond. At that point, we have the power to consciously leave our bodies and transcend this material world. But if we then come back for the purpose of helping others spiritually, and yet we ourselves have no more karma, at that point we become avatars. Paramahansa Yogananda said that he himself was an avatar because he came back for that purpose. Mahavatar Babaji would be an avatar who attained that status long ago and has received a dispensation from Cosmic Spirit to remain incarnate, that is, in a form on earth, but in a hidden way, for the purpose of helping the spirituality of mankind."*

Thus sitting on my bed in Tokyo, following my morning meditation, I picked up Yogananda's book and opened to a discussion of Babaji which included the following:

> *"Whenever anyone utters with reverence the name of Babaji, that devotee attracts an instant spiritual blessing."*

I thought; why not try to connect with him? I mentally called his name three times. Within twenty seconds, a powerful flood of energy entered my body, and light filled my head. I could feel the warm presence of his love and a sweet melting in my heart.

I could not believe what was happening to me. I had never had such powerful *darshan*[2] from a nonphysical being. Maharishi Mahesh Yogi had already made a deep impression on me each time I was in his presence, and on one occasion I almost fainted in front of him, but there was no one visible in my Tokyo room, and I had simply said a few words in my head!

Meeting Babaji in this way was the turning point that gave me some hope. Although I was still depressed, this miracle indicated recovery was possible, and I began to look for other signs and opportunities to carry me to a better place.

I still meditated twice a day, but somehow my meditation practice did not seem effective in this case. At that point I had practiced meditating for seventeen years, and its benefits formed a foundation that during that awful year kept me plodding along, working weekdays. Integrating other world-views, including meditation practices, doesn't automatically make one immune from getting depressed or falling into ruts. With the adoption of a different perspective, however, we may redefine ourselves; but even finding a good spiritual path doesn't mean we are 100% protected from the blows of major life changes. As Maharishi himself pointed out, there is no single universal cure-all fix-all for all times, events, and circumstances; and even he experienced reversals resulting from past karma.

I was not immune to the pitfall of being overly attached to my own worldview. As I outlined in my previous book, *Seraphim Blueprint: The Power of Angel Healing*, I assiduously practiced Transcendental Meditation up through the time that I had my mid-life crisis. And it was only with the help of another American, whom I met in Tokyo that I began to see that there were situations in which one could actually over-meditate

---

[2] There is no English equivalent to the Sanskrit word *darshan*. The term refers to the fact that when we are in the presence of a truly enlightened being, we receive some of his or her enlightened and enlightening energies as a free gift.

at the expense of one's well-being.

Stewart was that American who one day phoned me to inquire about attending meetings of the Tokyo Leisure Club (TLC), a club that I had founded that spring, as another means of escaping depression. We held our meetings in my spacious living room in Yoyogi Uehara, a lovely part of Tokyo I was lucky to reside in. These events attracted mostly foreigners living in Japan, and the meetings involved interesting speakers, either on political or spiritual topics. A few years later this club evolved into the Tokyo Circle of Light, founded in 1989, which monthly served the foreign community for the next twenty years.

Stewart, even in that first telephone conversation, impressed me with his knowledge of healing. His sense of humor and intelligence quickly put me at ease, so that without having even met him, I felt comfortable enough to talk about my depression and my physical problems.

He lived near me in Tokyo, and when we met, he demonstrated his skills in understanding the causes of my chronic health condition. He became my new mentor, who cracked open what at that time had become my rigid belief system based on Transcendental Meditation. He showed me that if I stopped meditating, my health would actually improve—something that was counterintuitive, both then and now.[3] I tested this theory by meditating regularly for one week, then stopping for a week. When I had done this alternately

---

[3] In the TM teaching, students are instructed that when a meditator is ill, he or she should meditate only "as much as is comfortable". When some malady (in TM parlance "heavy unstressing") is present, the stress-releasing powers of meditation can speed up the process of "purification" or normalization" to the point of causing actual discomfort and even disorientation. Thus, in extreme and unusual circumstances such as these, the teacher will sometimes have the meditator cut back the number of minutes of meditation until the illness or other symptoms have been resolved. However, stopping completely is not considered necessary except in the most intractable of circumstances, in which case, meditation can possibly be replaced with simple "body-feeling".

for about a month, and noticed how my overall well-being improved each time I stopped, I took a two-year break from meditation.

As a result of this shake-up, and realizing I was no longer "on the program" as meditators came to refer to their practice, I became open to other practices. This openness was greatly assisted by the addition of a divination tool—a pendulum, which Stewart provided, as part of my new training with the *School*, as this small esoteric school that we were part of was called. To this day I consider Stewart to be one of the most influential mentors in my life. He helped me to integrate my ethereal energies with the real world. He also opened me up to many New Age modalities that I previously thought were not as valuable as Transcendental Meditation. Through Stewart's guidance, I got to explore and experiment with them.

I began my research immediately. As a part-time university lecturer, I had time to practice the correct use of a pendulum as a divination tool. The pendulum I used was an egg-shaped stone dangling from a silver chain about seven inches long. Its 'answers' consisted of a few motions. A clockwise swing indicated a 'yes'. A counterclockwise swing indicated a 'no'. It occasionally just swung straight back and forth after I queried it, and that seemed to indicate 'do not know'.

I practiced for six months until I was certain that the answers I received were more than fifty percent correct. This I judged from the way events unfolded, as well as the way my body responded to therapies recommended by the pendulum. Of course, the pendulum was still limited by the way I framed my questions, but I was creative and often came up with new ways to query it.

In that first year of use, I didn't think of the pendulum as a psychic tool. It never occurred to me that I might be psychic. Instead, I thought of it as an extension

It never occurred to me that I might be psychic.

of my nervous system, much like my body was a computer with hidden files that I could now access. In my exposure to Transcendental Meditation training, I had been told that most of us are only using a small portion of our full mental potential. Thus, with pendulum use, I simply thought I was accessing more of my brain cells, resulting in fairly accurate information about my own bodily workings and needs.

That year my teaching schedule was light, and my curiosity strong. I played with the pendulum every morning. I would ask it innumerable questions—especially concerning my love life. Although I was usually inaccurate, with practice I noticed improvement. In a few months, I was astonished by the amount of information I received, information that turned out to be correct.

The pendulum's outward simplicity was deceptive. When suspended from my hand, it became a sensitive device, readily accessing cellular and neuronal information—even capable of retrieving data at a distance. In my case, its accuracy was further enhanced by years of meditation and clean living. I began calling it the "Cosmic Computer".

According to the English School, the metaphysical school located in Yeovil, Somerset, England, that Stewart had introduced me to, the pendulum received data through the sixth chakra via a meridian that connects the brow chakra with the muscles in the arm holding the chain. Stewart also told me that the sixth chakra bypassed the confusing internal dialogue of the conscious thinking process. Instead it allowed for intelligence stored in each and every cell to come out "louder" than the conscious mind, giving intuitive information startling in its frequent accuracy. The English School simply informed us that the pendulum accesses "cellular information". This sounded somewhat reasonable at the time, and I provisionally went with it. Introduction to the world of the pendulum came at a most beneficial juncture in my life. Not only did it provide some relief from my health problems, it ended a melancholic chapter, and set the stage for a new calling.

When I asked questions about my health, the pendulum liberated me from having to contact friends for advice; something I routinely used to do because of my lifelong indecisiveness. Since I was still in Tokyo, thousands of miles away from my friends—and in those days international telephone calls were very expensive—the pendulum proved to be quite useful indeed.

For several years following the initial thrill of having more access to hidden information through the pendulum, I assumed that I was receiving such information through some form of collective consciousness with no specific entities involved. But actually, Babaji had been around me off and on for some time after I first called him that May, waiting for me to recognize him. Later, he told me that he was relieved when I finally made a conscious connection with him, although that connection was tenuous at best. It was as if I had put some kindling on a small pile of wood and had lit it with a match, while he was fanning the flames. He was waiting for the fires of my spirituality to take hold, so I could be an instrument for his work. At that time, I didn't know how long he had been waiting, or that he had been waiting at all. For me, in this lifetime, it was all new and unbelievable.

This spiritual meeting with Babaji signaled a huge change in my life, which resulted in a completely new theory about souls: the theory of multiple souls that I am now offering.

Over that summer, my experience of Babaji's energies slowly faded, and I just assumed that my experience of him that May had been a singular event. I was wrong, but I wouldn't know that for several more years.

Chapter 5

Reading Past Lives

By early 1988, a year after my mother passed away, my emotions had stabilized, and I was still teaching English and history in Tokyo. I had come to trust my abilities with the pendulum, so that when a close Japanese girlfriend, Emiko, mentioned that her mother was hospitalized with cancer, I asked my friend if she would mind if I tried to heal her mother. She appreciated my offer and told me to proceed.

Although my friend's mother's condition was a painful reminder of my recent experience with my own mother, this time, as I used the pendulum, I felt the stirring of some new abilities. I had used the pendulum to assess Emiko's mother's condition with her photograph, since photographs hold a tremendous amount of psychic information about a person.

After checking in with her mother's energy almost daily via the photo, I became aware that she would not survive her sixtieth birthday. Before her death, however, I asked questions through the pendulum about when this woman had made the decision to die, because I believed then, and still do now, that a person subconsciously orchestrates their own well-being and time of departure.

I knew from my girlfriend that her mother's relationship with her husband had been difficult; therefore, I expected an answer indicating that she had made the decision to die at some time during her long marriage. Some believe that cancer can be an expression of a repressed wish for a divorce. In Japan (and in many other cultures as well) separating through death is much more socially acceptable than getting a divorce, even an amicable one. But to my surprise, as I went backwards by decades, I found that her decision to die at this time had actually been made before she was born!

I was getting this information from simply swinging my pendulum with my right hand while touching her forehead in her photograph with my left forefinger. Since I had scanned her whole life span by going back to her birth and was still getting a 'no' answer, I asked on a whim if hers had been a pre-birth decision, and got a 'yes' answer from the pendulum. It struck me immediately that I must have access to data beyond what is stored in human tissue. Still not considering the possibility that I might be psychic, I knew that in the East Indian tradition, pre-birth knowledge signified access to the so-called "Akashic records". The Sanskrit word *Akasha* refers to the astral plane, and according to ancient Indian sources, the astral plane is the literal storehouse of accounts of all present, past, and future events. At the time, I imagined that only Vedic seers and the most accomplished of psychics had access to such records.

I was overwhelmed. I began testing to see if I had access to my own past lives, as well as the past lives of close friends, and got the most interesting answers. I called Stewart that day to get his opinion as to what all this might mean. I asked him if he could access the Akashic records through his pendulum. When he answered "No" and added that he did not person-ally know of other users of the pendulum who could do so, I was quite surprised. He concluded our conversation with, "I guess you have found a new profession—you can now call yourself a Past-Life Reader. You can make $1000 an hour doing that." A typical Stewart opinion—seeing the market value in everything.

Life went on as usual. I taught my college classes. Occasionally, at a party I would discover people who had previously received a past-life reading from a professional psychic. Then I would offer to do a casual past-life reading for them, as well, taking my pendulum out of my pocket, where it usually resided, and asking them not to tell me in advance what the other reader had said about their past lives. At such a party I would mentally ask how many past lives the partygoer had had and what the most significant past life had been, in which part of the world it had been located, and in what century or millennium this might have been. I would also ask whether the significance of such a life was based on the manner of birth or death, a relationship with someone they knew in this lifetime, or a special talent or ability they'd had previously and that might be important in their current life. This would take me about five minutes, and I seemed to have no problem with doing it in a noisy environment. Afterwards, I compared my reading to their earlier one. When on three different occasions my perceptions corresponded favorably with their previous readings, I began to accept that I had some ability as a past-life reader. When friends of friends began calling me for readings, I gained more confidence. Still, I did not intend to become a professional reader, as even with this experience, I lacked confidence, not having been trained by a professional, as well as not being especially gifted, or so I thought.

Then other events in my life propelled me to leave Japan, not for America, but for Australia. In order to augment my savings, I advertised my psychic abilities in an English language weekly newspaper, and in that first week scheduled appointments for ten people who answered my ad. The universe was definitely supporting my decision to become a professional psychic.

When a person would show up on my doorstep for a past-life reading, my methodology then and now is to simply ask for

ir full name and birth date. From that
r nt in the session and for the following
five or ten minutes, I go through several
steps to access their whole situation. First,
I want to know if they have angels in their
aura. This would be a team of angels that

> **Most people have three or four angels.**

supports them in their daily comings and goings, providing
luck, lessons, and guidance. Most people have three or four
angels surrounding them from birth. The type and number of
angels is significant. Usually, the more angels one has, the more
responsibility one has in the real world. When a person shows
up for a reading with about eight angels, I often assume they
are in the medical profession, and I am frequently correct.

After checking their aura for angels, spirit guides, negative
elementals, or lost souls, and also for negative thought-forms,
which form a slight crust around that person, I go on to check
on how many souls the person has. The number is usually two
to four souls. Then I determine where each soul originated.
This tells me much about that person. After that, I check which
is the birth-soul, which is usually alone in the body until about
the age of eleven. I would also check the dimensionality of
each soul, which is a grading system for souls (more on this
later). Then I ask the person to tell me why they wanted the
reading, and I psychically deal with any questions or issues
they had in their lives, swinging my pendulum for confirmation of any impressions I have. And then I ask each soul if it
is happy to be inside this person's body. If I get a 'no', then
I will ask the client if they have been experiencing depression, and if so for how many years, trying to confirm my own
analysis, that they are likely depressed. If they admit to being
depressed, I will suggest to them that my spirit guides and
I can alleviate this suffering by removing the depressed soul
from their body. If they consent to that procedure, I tell them
to simply close their eyes, that the process will take a minute
or so, and they might feel some tingling in their body.

But I see that I am getting ahead of the story here. In 1989, I gave clients only a past-life reading with no intervention of this kind.

One might wonder why I wasn't aware of my psychic abilities prior to the age of forty-five. With hindsight, I now understand why I was not only unaware of my own psychic gifts earlier in life, but how my lack of awareness may have been a form of denial. Of course, general lack of awareness of 'professional psychic' as a career choice could easily be blamed on school curriculums. It is difficult to choose something that's not on the "menu". In reality, though, many of us have been psychics before, in past lives. But these collective memories engender fear instead of joy because of the way we were treated in those lifetimes.

Exact figures are unknown, but in Europe in the past millennia, thousands, possibly hundreds of thousands, were burned at the stake as witches. And those who were not burned at the stake watched those who were, which also engendered a lasting fear in the majority of the world's population. A past-life memory of being burned as a witch could leave a slight charcoal taste in one's mouth upon thinking the word 'psychic'. At the very least, such an experience would serve as a prophylactic preventing reapplication for such employment.

And that is what happened in my own case. Although, I have had only occasional recall of my own past lives, mainly through dreams, and have no clear memories of being burned at the stake, when I asked about the possibility of such experiences through my pendulum, I have been told I was burned twice for such "heresies". Thus, in this lifetime, the long-term denial of my own psychic abilities, which didn't surface until I was forty-five, had subterranean reasons all along. On the plus side, perhaps, that fear engenders obsession with accuracy in my readings. I'd rather appear to be lacking in confidence, than to risk making any mistakes.

Chapter 6

The Discovery of Multiple Souls

Within a few months of beginning my public readings in Tokyo, a good friend and longtime student of esoteric matters, René Breuls, an expatriate Dutchman, introduced me to the idea that, while most human souls originated on this planet, a small percentage of souls came from other parts of our galaxy, or even other galaxies. These "seed souls", he said, were sent here thousands of years ago to help raise the vibration of human beings. He called them "Wanderers". Then he went on to describe them:

In their galaxy they do not have male nor female beings, but are asexual. Thus, when they come here, they are confused by human sexuality. Since, upon arriving, they must incarnate into one of our bodies, they make an arbitrary choice, although they are rarely comfortable being either male or female. They are also less than enthusiastic about our mating processes, or by the idea of raising children. They express this in their lives by trying to avoid, or postpone, marriage, or readily divorcing once married. Their role on our planet is similar to that of missionaries. They are in service to primitive Earth. They are more or less on autopilot. In each new incarnation on Earth, they have to rediscover their foreign origin, as they are just as perplexed as any of us as to why they feel so lonely here.

Since, on the cellular level, they unconsciously know that this is not their original home, they are a bit confused. Furthermore, they have no one they can turn to for advice.

With every descriptive sentence about these star souls, or 'Wanderers', as he called them, I couldn't help but think he was talking about me. He said that only a small percentage of Earth's population fits this category—possibly 65 million people.

His air of certainty about this and other esoteric matters perplexed me. He was a businessman, representing a large American chemical company in Tokyo. He had a way of stating things with unquestionable authority. When I asked him about his sources, he said over the years he had read widely on esoteric matters.

As soon as I was alone, after saying goodbye to René, I tried to verify the existence of Wanderers psychically. Yes, I was told there is such a category of souls. However, they were much more plentiful than he'd thought, maybe as much as thirteen percent of the world's population. I also psychically confirmed my suspicion that I was among their ranks.

Soon thereafter, I was ready to test this new theory with clients coming to me for past-life readings. I began making this differentiation of soul types in 1989. Thus, when I saw new clients, I would determine initially whether a client's soul was from another star—a Wanderer—or from this planet—an Earthling. Each time I discovered that a client was an Earthling; I would tell them that they were normal in their desire to form a family and have children. Almost without fail, they would affirm that they held these desires. Wanderers, however, would be amazed when I went through the characteristics that René had delineated. They, too, would confirm that my statements about them were true. For another six months, these two categories, Earthlings and Wanderers, proved to be adequate for all of my readings.

Then one day, a client came to me, and when I asked my guidance for their soul origin, I was told that the client was from this planet, as well as from a different star system. This was perplexing. I kept repeating the question for clarification. Determined to get a 'correct' answer, I rechecked my own energy, knowing that I could possibly be too tired to get a correct answer, and thus my 'yes's' and 'no's' could be switched. But I confirmed that I was indeed grounded enough to get a valid response, and thus I could trust this new level of complexity.

After the client left, I began to do a reading on my own soul situation. Again, I appeared to be a test case of this split development. In other words, I also had two origins in the universe. At that time, I was thinking in percentages of one soul—maybe fifty-fifty or forty-sixty. For a few months, I continued to work with this new idea, which I called 'split souls'.

Then, about a month later, a novel development caused me to tweak the new information a bit more. One day, during the course of a client's reading, I asked about the number of past lives of this split-souled client, and I received two different numbers—seventy-two past lives and one hundred and fifty-three past lives. Shocked by this, I checked again several times if my own energy was balanced. Yes, I felt that my energy was working correctly. This was the beginning of the feeling that the 'split' soul might actually be two souls inhabiting the same body. Still hardly believing what was coming through to me, I withheld this information from the client involved, wanting to make double-sure by checking once more in private.

The more I worked with this idea psychically, however, the more confirmation I was given for the possibility that two souls can exist harmoniously in one body. Getting responses like this from my spirit guide (whoever he or she was, as I was still unaware that I even had a resident spirit guide, but trusted that with my clean living and meditation experience, somebody 'up there" was assisting me), I felt cut loose from reality—like a cog spinning freely. I knew I was in uncharted waters, especially because of my academic background. I was familiar with cultural values from many civilizations throughout recorded history, but I could not recall anything like this in Asian or Western civilization, or in religious studies. (Many years later, to my surprise, I discovered an entry for "Multiple Souls" in the *Encyclopedia Britannica*, of all places, which stated that this belief exists widely in traditional Southeast Asian, Indonesian, and Mongolian cultures.)

Something that troubled me in those early days was that such a split internal situation might be confused with what was commonly known as 'multiple personalities' or 'dissociative personality disorder'. When I considered my own two souls, however, I realized that although I had had some trouble with decision making over the years, I had generally functioned well with this handicap—or possibly, blessing. Most of my twin-souled clients also seemed to be performing quite satisfactorily in the world, so I suspected that I was dealing with a previously unknown phenomenon. Since this issue was central to my work, however, it was important to delineate the differences between multiple souls and dissociative personality disorder.

I spent the next six months finding more than one soul in some of my clients' bodies, while I wrestled with the veracity of what I was finding. I needed to resolve in my own mind if what I was discovering was multiple personality disorder, schizophrenia, or something truly different. At the time, I had only the haziest ideas of what these psychological disorders were, and later discovered that most people form their opinions about these disorders from classic movies they have seen, such as *Three Faces of Eve* and the book and television drama *Sybil*, based upon the true story of the life of Shirley Ardell Mason.

With some research, though, I discovered that schizophrenia is a common disorder, which, despite its name has nothing to do with split personalities, while multiple personality disorder is relatively rare. People confuse schizophrenia with multiple personality disorder because the prefix 'schizo-' means 'split'. In the case of schizophrenia, however, the split refers to the emotions being separate from rational thinking. 'Schizo' also refers to hearing voices in the head or seeing imagery, which appear to be distinct from one's own thoughts and external reality. The medical profession now regards schizophrenia as a chemical imbalance, and symptoms are often managed with drugs.

Since 1980, psychiatrists have officially recognized Multiple Personality Disorder (MPD), or as it is now sometimes called Dissociative Identity Disorder (DID) as a disease, most likely the result of childhood trauma. Recently, as the media have more openly discussed such issues, the reported cases of MPD have also increased. There are professional disputes about MPD because of its prevalence in a single country— the United States of America—which makes skeptics believe that it is simply a fad, and with less media attention it would disappear. In any case, it exists in the popular imagination, and thus it is important to separate this "condition" from the work being presented here.

Multiple Personality Disorder posits the existence of distinct personalities, often identified even with different names. Frequently, one of the personalities involved is childlike, because when traumatized early in life, the person "dissociated" from a traumatic reality in order to protect itself from that reality and then failed to mature normally. Then, dissociating from further traumatic experiences becomes a way of dealing with them, and in that way, multiple personalities become separate one from the others. The clearest indicator of this disorder, however, is the experience of memory loss, or amnesia, with each personality hardly willing to recognize the experiences, or sometimes even the existence, of the other personalities in the body. The symptoms can also include depression, panic attacks, and inability to function in society. MPD is always associated with co-morbidity or more commonly known psychological disorders.

In 1989, when I was pondering these issues, I recognized that the twin-soul phenomenon was superficially similar to MPD in that several souls take turns governing the body. With the several-souls scenario, however, the sequential control of the body is fixed for much longer periods than those associated with MPD—normally about two years for each soul, but this sequence can also be as short as six months. When a different soul takes over, there could be a personality change, but it is usually a subtle shift, hardly recognized by the individual involved. One of the most significant differences between MPD and twin-souls, however, is the lack of amnesia in the twin-soul scenario. With twin-souls, the souls involved are aware of the total life experience of the whole being through time. Also, as I noted over time, my twin-souled clients never mentioned childhood trauma. The second—and crucially important—difference between MPD and multiple souls is that MPD, as noted above, is always associated with co-morbidity. People with multiple souls, in my experience at least, do not have serious psychoses.

Thus, before I left Japan for new adventures abroad, I had already found that the idea of twin-souls was most likely distinct from any known psychological maladies. I became more confident in talking to people who approached me for help with their twin-soul situation, and I often received confirmation from them that I was on the right track. What was surprising at the time was that most of them readily accepted this new theory to be accurately describing their own life situation.

Then I made the decision not to return to America, but to head south for a new adventure in Sydney, Australia. One of my close friends in Tokyo was returning to his favorite place on the planet, and he invited me to come Down Under.

I left Japan in March of 1990, and liked Sydney enough to establish residence there. I lived off my savings and occasionally did past-life readings for friends. In the following few months I discovered that some people had four souls in their bodies. I was shocked by this development, but still it didn't appear to be too problematic in their situations, therefore I glossed over them.

Without having a good handle on the phenomenon, I was still insecure in focusing on this multi-souled aspect of my readings. I was trying to learn from others what it meant to have more than one soul in a body. When I was still in Tokyo, I had seen many healthy twin-souled clients. I congratulated them on their variety of talents and smoothed over their relationship difficulties. With the passage of time, however, increasingly difficult cases were appearing, though still I saw few serious problems, other than complexity, and advised them to accept their complex fate when they were obviously having conflicting desires.

Fortuitously, I found a new colleague in 1990 with whom I could discuss such questions. Various events conspired to bring about our collaboration, and without this serendipitous encounter, the whole subject of soul surgery would have tarried a bit longer in the astral plane.

A rabbit arranged for our meeting.

Chapter 7

Refining the Theory:
A Fortuitous Meeting

In Tokyo I had a rabbit companion named Butsi. Previously I had been a cat person, but when Butsi came into my life, I saw the incredible joy he contained. As a small bunny, Butsi darted in ten directions at once, and seemed to have endless affection for me. Somehow I felt that I knew Butsi from a previous human incarnation. He seemed to be consoling me for my mother's death. That a human soul would choose to incarnate as a companion animal for such a short life puzzled me, but I came to accept the likelihood that, due to strong love, a soul could devise special means to be at a certain place and time, even if it was only for a short while.

With my move to Australia, however, I was forced to leave Butsi behind—although in good hands, of course. Australia, being free of many animal diseases, including rabies, has strict barriers to importing animals. Besides, Australians, once having introduced rabbits, came to regret it, as their country became overrun with rabbits to the detriment of their agriculture.

I tried living without any pets for a while. After not seeing a rabbit for four months, however, I was thrilled when an acquaintance mentioned that a nearby Italian café kept one that ran freely among the guests in an enclosed rear garden.

I soon went to see this rabbit and became attached to her. It was a long walk to visit her, but I justified it by the thought that she needed my weekly healing. In reality, it was a mutual healing.

One Sunday, a regular patron at the café came over to ask what I was doing with my hands resting on the rabbit's head. When I explained that I was helping the rabbit recover from the café's jarring energy, she left her table of friends and joined me. She began saying how much she loved this rabbit, and then went on to ask about my healing abilities. I explained that I had a natural gift for healing and was very attached to rabbits.

Sharon then introduced herself, and mentioned that as a child she was clairvoyant and could see angelic beings and *devas*.[4] She was originally from Scotland, the daughter of a career military officer, and had lived all over the world. By the age of thirteen, though, she found the military lifestyle not suitable to her hippie tendencies. When she could no longer bear it, she ran away from home, and then became a single mom at fifteen.

Still, she led a clean lifestyle until she was eighteen, when she met and married a charismatic abuser. She joined him in various addictions that resulted in the shutdown of her visionary abilities. When I met her at thirty-two, she was still using some drugs, but was in a satisfactory relationship with a new partner.

For whatever reason, when Sharon met me, she was eager to turn her life around. She somehow sensed that I could help. The next day we again met at the café by coincidence, and she told me it was her birthday. As a birthday gift, I gave her a past-life reading right there in the courtyard.

I discovered that Sharon was a single-souled Earthling. I

---

[4] In the Vedic literature, devas are deities representing the forces of nature. Some represent moral values.

also ascertained that she was a natural channeler and would probably be capable of automatic writing (in the psychic sense) within about two years. Her seventh chakra was shut down back then, which was blocking her innate abilities. For this problem I instructed her in the use of a white light visualization exercise to heal the nonfunctioning chakra, by simply imagining a hot, white ball of light coming into the top of her head, healing and warming that area for about five minutes each time.

"If you do this exercise daily for a month, the chakra will clear." I encouraged her to learn how to use a pendulum as a psychic tool. She then asked me if I would teach her how to use it correctly, and I agreed to instruct her. Quickly, she cleared her seventh chakra, and became quite proficient in using a pendulum. She seemed to want to make up for lost time, and the pendulum appeared to be virtually attached to her right hand all day long from that point on.

One night, following a visit to my apartment, Sharon went home to continue using the pendulum into the night, since her best connection with her newfound spirit guides was around midnight. This particular night, however, something unusual occurred. She relayed this to me the next morning on the phone.

"Last night after your lesson, I continued to work with the pendulum when suddenly I found I was communicating with a new entity."

"How can you tell it was somebody new talking to you?" I inquired.

"The feeling of the pendulum changes. The swing quickens, or slows. The crystal feels heavier, or lighter. This entity was definitely powerful and at ease communicating with me through the pendulum. I'm pretty sure it wasn't one of my regular guides. He wanted me to call him an 'Earth Guardian'."

This new possibility stretched my comprehension. Until then, my soul vocabulary was limited to Earthlings and Wanderers. I was still unaware that I, too, had spirit guides following me around. I couldn't imagine that Babaji, after healing me in Tokyo, would have continued to be with me in Sydney, or even that he was with me at all beyond those first ten minutes of my incredible experience with him in 1987, which was three years prior to this experience in Australia. When using my pendulum, I simply thought I was tapping into cellular information, or—erroneously as it turned out—my Higher Self, which I vaguely equated with being one of my souls back then.

Sharon continued, "It was so much fun talking to him. He constantly made me laugh. He was so powerful and uplifting. I could have talked with him all night. As it was, we spoke for about four hours."

"Why did he call himself an Earth Guardian?"

"He and about seven other Earth Guardians are responsible for maintaining peace and tranquility on the planet. I hope that I can contact him again. He was so wise and all-knowing. I felt as if we were becoming great buddies."

I had little to comment on this event. As Sharon's tutor, I remained skeptical of her abilities. Although part of me was intimidated by this development, another part was open to learning from the situation. Besides, she was rapidly becoming my friend. Even so, I thought, if there are Earth Guardians responsible for maintaining peace and tranquility on the planet, they weren't doing an especially great job.

My first visit to Sharon's home later that same day almost banished my doubts. I also got to meet her partner Sean and her daughter Tracy. Poverty and the destitute homeless characterized her Eastern suburbs neighborhood known as Woolloomooloo. Approaching her house, I could feel the general malaise of the area. Once Sharon opened her front door, however, and I stepped into the large front room, I immediately felt a high energy remaining from whatever spirit had been there the night before. It felt like entering a sunny garden where all the devas and nature spirits had been playing. I told her that the energy lingering there was incredible.

"Yes. Isn't it something else?" Sharon brightly responded standing there in her dance tights.

But that same night Sharon's rapid opening to the forces of light had a strange consequence. When I called her the next morning, her partner, Sean, answered the phone with a weary, "I don't think Sharon is up to talking to you now. She'll call you when she is."

A few minutes later a rather sleepy Sharon returned my call. "Ruth, I haven't been able to sleep all night. Some spirit, whom I first thought to be the Earth Guardian, kept bothering me. But this entity's energy is really different from that of the Earth Guardian—much more negative."

"What happened?" I asked.

"Look, we are all still really frightened. We don't know what to do to get rid of it. Do you have any good ideas?"

Even without doing a psychic reading, I thought a lost soul was involved. In the dozens of people I had previously taught, Sharon was the first to be attacked psychically. I was unprepared, and lacked experience as an exorcist (I hadn't even seen the movie). Still, I did have one idea.

"It is best that you get out of the house as quickly as you can. Let's meet at the rabbit café in an hour, and I will do a full reading there."

We met outside in the café's sunny garden. Sharon looked undressed without her usual heavy silver jewelry. "What happened to all your jewelry?"

"The spirit directed me to take it all off, except it wanted me to wear this small cross. You see, at first I thought it was the Earth Guardian merely helping in my purification process. I thought that because he wanted me to wear a cross, he was a good spirit. But then he told me to dress all in black. And then he wouldn't let me sleep, and he began to feel increasingly negative."

"Well, let me take a few minutes to do a psychic reading now," I said. My pendulum indicated that the spirit attacking Sharon was an old Irishman who had died of natural causes. Although he had been quietly resting in one of her closets for thirty years, the high energy bestowed upon the house by the Earth Guardian's spirit had awakened this Rip Van Winkle, bringing him out of the closet.

Unaware of his own death, he began pestering Sharon to find his best mate. Since Sharon was able to understand him, this only reinforced his feeling that he was alive. Therefore, he continued to exhort her to help him. More confused than malicious, by tapping into the Earth guardian's enlivening energies, the ghost had become capable of wreaking havoc.

I relayed the information that I was receiving to Sharon, and she thought it was plausible. I then asked through the pendulum what we should do, and was told that I needed to perform a *puja* to send the spirit home.

Trained as a teacher of Transcendental Meditation, I had never heard that the initiation ceremony (called a *puja* in Sanskrit), which we used to teach new meditators, might double as a means of exorcism. I just intuitively knew it might do the job. According to tradition, this ancient ceremony invokes the enlightened consciousness of the yogic masters. The ceremony begins with the words, here translated from Sanskrit:

Whether pure or impure, whether all places are permeated by purity or impurity, whoever opens to the expanded vision of unbounded awareness gains inner and outer purity.

If the puzzle we faced required purification, then this ceremony seemed perfect.

Under ideal conditions, I probably would have searched for a "real" exorcist. But being new to Sydney, I had not yet had time to network. There seemed to be little choice but to go ahead as planned. Besides it was an exciting challenge. We did not discuss the possibility of failure and what that might mean.

I explained to Sharon what I thought should be the procedure for the day:

"I would like to perform a special Sanskrit ceremony in your bedroom at five o'clock. Until then, please don't return home. It would also be good if Sean and Tracey were to stay away, too. I need to practice the ceremony alone before then, as I am rusty. For the ceremony, I would like you to buy some fruit and flowers. Meet me with these at four-thirty at Café Hernandez [closer to my residence than the "rabbit café"] and we'll walk to your house together. When we get there, I want you to quickly change into all white clothing, or the closest to that color you have in your wardrobe."

The day was bright and sunny as I prepared. I also wore white while practicing the ceremony. I met Sharon and we walked to her home. Coming from the sunny street into the front room, it felt nothing like the day before. Now it was like walking into a cold fog, or giant freezer. Having read about this cold effect of ghostly presence, I was amazed at the actual experience.

"Sharon, show me your bedroom so I can set up for the ceremony." She led me upstairs to the front room, also icy cold.

"Can you go and change your clothes and wait in another bedroom until I've finished?" She nodded and left.

I worked as quickly as I could. I invited the ghost to sit in an empty chair nearby and watch as I recited the Sanskrit words of devotion. After the first two stanzas, I could feel the powerful uplifting effect indicative of a higher presence, and a foretaste of success.

When I finished singing, I called Sharon in to join me because she was clairvoyant and might see him departing. "Now let's get him to go to the Light."

Facing the empty chair I said, "You don't realize it, but you have been dead for thirty-odd years. And the mate you so strongly want to see again also died shortly after you did. It is now time for you to join him in the spirit world. Do you see a bright Light somewhere in this room? If you can, please follow the guide that will take you to that Light."

> You have been dead for thirty-odd years.

"Sharon, can you see anything happening? Is he going?"

"No," she replied.

So then we both tried to coax him with repeated soft words directing him to the Light. After about twenty minutes, she said, "He's taking a hand offered to him, and going towards the Light."

Slowly, the room warmed up, and I began to feel we had completed the process.

Thus ended my first exorcism.

To prevent future ghostly invasions, I pleaded with Sharon, "Please throw out all your second-hand clothing that might be harboring other ghosties." Later her guides also instructed her to perform purifying rites and general cleansing. She spent several days fulfilling these details. In addition, I gave her a trilogy of books by the noted Australian psychic Dawn Hill. Sharon was clearly an open channel, and Hill's books contained advice about spirit protection. From that point on, we both automatically recited Hill's prayer for protection before beginning any psychic work.

I call upon the spirit of God to stand guard at the doorway of my soul and protect me from deceit and deception, and ʉide me down the path of love, Light and truth. I will ʉmmit myself to the Light.

Protection from invasion by spirits and avoidance of psychic attack by living and non-living beings had become a necessary aspect of working in this psychic/spiritual realm. Initially, my many hours of daily meditation had obviated the need for any type of personal protection. After this event with Sharon, though, my guides felt it was necessary for me to experience a couple of psychic attacks personally. They were underscoring the importance of the experience and the need to mention protective procedures to future students.

Visualizing white light, especially in a counter-clockwise spiraling conical form, has become an important way of sealing my aura. Before leaving home I often close down my top four chakras visualizing them initially as open lotus flowers and then gradually closing the petals tightly.

As a result of the exorcism performed in her house, Sharon chose to transform herself immediately. The following day she gave up smoking cigarettes and marijuana, as well as drinking coffee and alcohol.

At the time I had never heard of a person giving up so many addictions simultaneously, so I was a bit skeptical, expecting her to backslide within a few weeks. I was wrong. For many years now, Sharon has not relapsed. Later, when I questioned her about how she could give up so many habits all at once, she replied, "I asked my guides to take away all the withdrawal symptoms in exchange for my doing full-time spiritual work. They have kept their part of the bargain, and so have I."

After several weeks and to my great relief, Sharon remained free from reinvasion. Next, she mystified me with claims that she had an ability to clear lost souls from people's auras with the help of her guides. Sharon was a seer from birth, with a long dormant period. Maybe she was truly gifted. She was such an interesting character, and I was enjoying her company immensely. We had determined by then that we must have known each other in past lives, because we felt so close to each other, even though we came from vastly dissimilar back-grounds.

Sharon really threw herself into her spiritual work. She claimed to be clearing hundreds of lost souls from the astral plane. I had little means of judging her ability; I thought that her ego was controlling her actions, and that she might be competing with me. In situations like this, where skepticism and emotions are involved, I had trouble asking my guidance for answers, and thus was prevented from getting an accurate intuitive reading. In such cases, I was forced to let the passage of time reveal the answers.

The day that I truly felt Sharon had unique abilities came a month later. While visiting me at home, she suddenly said, "There is a lost soul in your aura. Let me take it off you."

"Sure, go ahead."

After she made some gesture indicating she was removing it, she said, "It has been with you for at least ten years. No wonder you have had a chronic physical problem." She then attempted to channel some healing energy to the affected area. As she worked on me, I felt nothing. By the next morning, however, I was feeling considerably lighter and happier. I finally acknowledged Sharon's ability to remove lost souls. Personal experience is the ultimate test. With all my intuition and experience in meditation, I had still been at a loss to identify this particular long-term major drain on my energy. Sharon released in a few seconds what had gone undetected for years. Further confirmation came when my health began to improve noticeably from that day.

Since the pendulum had become a permanent fixture in Sharon's life, I worried that she would burn out, as she literally worked round-the-clock, even clearing souls in her dreams while she slept. She relayed stories of dark beings that tried to prevent her from doing her work as she rested. They attempted to trick her by fanning her own personal fears. She once mentioned being attacked by an incubus (a demonic sexual entity) as she slept. By this time, we were talking daily about all the souls she was clearing.

It seemed that the more she worked in clearing them, the more new ones she attracted. She picked them up in her favorite coffee shops in King's Cross, an inner suburb of Sydney, or simply by walking down the street. She constantly chanted a Latin mantra to herself as part of the clearing process. Once I accepted the validity of what she was doing, she began sharing more of her internal experiences with me:

"A week ago I had to pick lost souls off of people individually. But this past week I am flat out [exhausted] from clearing souls that are lining up in the astral plane where they are in limbo. I don't know how many hundreds I have cleared. The other souls that I have sent to the Light must have advertised my abilities because they are now coming to me in droves!"

Later she reported, "I seem to have finished clearing the willing group. For now, I am coming across a much more resistant bunch. Since these newer ones were being so un-cooperative in the beginning, I was threatening them with a lightning bolt. When they didn't take my threat seriously, I zapped them. I was actually surprised when they completely vanished. After I demonstrated this a few times, now all I have to do is threaten to zap them and they go running to the Light. I am somewhat relieved in that I don't have to zap them anymore, because I feel now that I was incurring serious karma by extinguishing their souls." I told her I thought she was right and needed to tone things down.

I was shocked by her behavior. Zapping souls did not sound karmically clean to me. Both of us were learning on the job, or more probably remembering such abilities from past-life experience. We inevitably made mistakes. Even though Sharon was clearing myriads of souls, she still found that occasionally a more powerful demonic force would attack her psychically.

In the few cases when this happened, she would endure the situation as long as she could, trying to handle it in her own way. When she could no longer bear the torment, she would ask me for help. I would then perform a *puja*, as it seemed to clear out the intruders.

Finally, I instructed Sharon in Transcendental Meditation, so that she could protect herself and clear some of the stress she was incurring in this process. She loved the meditation and did it faithfully thereafter.

When doing work involving soul rescue, it is often good to have a partner, as one can never be certain of the unseen forces at work. Also it is somehow easier to have a friend to keep a check on one's sanity. I was especially good at identifying unusual entities that showed up around us. For some odd reason, once we could name the intruder, the battle was more than half won. The childhood ditty "Sticks and stones will break my bones, but names will never hurt me" was turned on its head. Instead, once the guides knew that I could name the being involved, they could take remedial action. At the time, the work appeared to require this type of partnership.

One day Sharon came over to my apartment for a social visit. It was a special treat to have her over because she rarely had the time away from her gym practice and her daily chores. "So tell me how you first got introduced to the pendulum," she asked.

I hardly ever thought about my interaction with Babaji. When I learned to use the pendulum in Tokyo, the English School that trained me in its use simply informed us that the pendulum accesses cellular information. And I never thought to doubt it. The School didn't tell us that we could pick up spirit guides through using the pendulum.

Once I discovered that I had access to the Akashic records through the pendulum, I still didn't make an association with Babaji. The English School had informed me that I might have an "ally" in my aura. When I asked Stewart about the meaning of their word "ally", he said it could mean a spirit guide. I thought it was possibly Babaji, but I still didn't feel that I had a special connection to him.

When I told Sharon about the Tokyo experience with Babaji, she told me that he had never left me. I was still skeptical, though, because of feeling unworthy of any continual contact with him. After all, Yogananda, only had rare contact, as was true of his guru as well.

Sharon suddenly interrupted me as I spoke: "He's here, right now!"

"What? That can't be!" I cried.

Swinging her pendulum, she replied, "Look, he's talking to me as we speak. He's saying he has been with you all along."

I was skeptical, thrilled, and puzzled. But slowly the possibility that he might have become my personal spirit guide began to sink in. For several months, though, I asked through my pendulum almost daily if Babaji was with me. When I kept getting a strong "yes" answer, I began to feel tentatively that he indeed was with me. Occasionally I would get a "no" answer. It took a few more days to understand what had happened. Babaji's movements are all for a purpose. While generally present, he does leave occasionally. He can be in about two hundred places at once, but sometimes he needs to regroup his energies for an emergency elsewhere; thus he leaves. Devotees in India frequently call him, and I have noted his absence when there is a political upheaval there.

Over the next few years, I queried other spiritual mentors regarding Babaji. They all confirmed his presence with me. I still didn't understand why Babaji was by my side. Gradually, I began to think his presence was related to teaching me about the multiple-soul phenomenon.

By this time Sharon and I had become a team. Our mutual guides networked with each other, so that if, on a particular day, I found someone who had a lost soul attached, Babaji would alert me, and then remove the soul from the subject, imprisoning it in a corner of my apartment. Souls would be detained there, not bothering me, until the next time I spoke with Sharon by phone. Then, I would give her the names of the people who'd had the lost souls attached to them, and she would simply receive the lost souls through the phone line and then clear them at her leisure.

Working as a team, Sharon and I combined our psychic understanding and theories. I supplied her with my broad-brush ideas concerning soul origins and soul crowding. She filled in some important details with the help of her guide, whom she called "Mark Adam". Although I had detected up to four souls in a few clients before, I was uncomfortable with the idea of more than two. Mark Adam relayed that there could be three, five, or even six souls in a body, and he referred to the phenomenon as "multiple-souls". Before hearing this, I had been talking about 'double-souls' or 'twin-souls'. Odd numbers of souls and the possibility of six-souled individuals was a shock to me. Initially, I resisted these ideas. Soon, however, I was also finding people with five and six souls. I researched historical geniuses, like Mozart and Einstein, and, using my pendulum, I found that they had four souls each. I was being forced to recognize this phenomenon as an important issue. Sharon and I were daily discussing matters related to multiple souls.

Under the Influence of an Elemental

Every couple of weeks we were adding to our list of possible types of disembodied entities. The "lost soul" was the most common. Sharon brought up the idea of 'elementals'— entities representing the elements of fire, air, earth, and water, which had long been recognized in European culture. Sharon resurrected them from the dustbins of history, so that they would once again become part of our modern vocabulary.

These entities had fallen from grace. They expressed their fallen state by being mischievous—attacking a person while he or she was sleeping, or keeping them stuck with certain bad habits. It often took Sharon a day and a night to clear an elemental, while it took her only a few minutes to clear a lost soul. Unlike the human lost souls, elementals were not directed to the Light; instead, we restored them to their proper devic form. Then they could again be responsible for a particular garden, if it was an earth elemental, or a particular lake, if it was a water elemental. In their fallen state, they presented themselves to Sharon as gnarled and ugly. When she was able to "turn" them, they again became large, beautiful, and unique male and female non-physical beings.

How had they fallen from grace? Sharon felt they had become displaced by human activities. For example, when real estate developers drain ponds, and erect buildings, they inevitably uproot water elementals.

Extraterrestrials & Interdimensionals

The next type of being that put in an appearance was the 'extraterrestrial'. Since Sharon was attracting so many souls, and her aura was about three-stories high with forty-four angels in attendance, any entity with awareness of other planes would find her in a crowd. The extraterrestrials were no exception. To us, they were insidious enigmas.

Sharon turned to me for help whenever one appeared. She wanted to know why they were hanging around, and what she was to do about them. Most of the time, these entities were simply observing her techniques, then reporting back to their civilizations about what she could accomplish. We had initially surmised that Sharon was about one of eight people on the planet with such extraordinary talents. Certainly she attracted astral and extraterrestrial attention.

Then the final unusual entity emerged. This was what I called an 'interdimensional' or 'dimensional being', a being that had never been human but had come here directly from another civilization in a different dimension. My guides had told me that there are about thirty-two dimensions encircling any particular

> There are about thirty-two dimensions encircling any particular planet...

planet, so the possible sources of such beings are many. For example, one such soul could be from the ninth dimension of a Pleiadian planet. When they put in an appearance in the third dimension their mission was usually observation.

In one instance, an interdimensional being was draining Sharon's energy, and we could think of no way to dislodge it. I simply told Sharon that it intended to stay with her as an observer for about a day and a half and that she should humor him, and he would eventually leave of his own accord. That is what she did. Much later I discovered that these beings mainly had an angelic vibration and that their presence was most auspicious.

I remember one fine spring day in Sydney, when Sharon and I decided to take a stroll in the lush Royal Botanical Garden near the harbor. As we walked along admiring the flowers, Sharon was chanting and swinging her pendulum and every so often discovering a misplaced elemental embedded in a stone sculpture. She would extract it from the stone and then initiate its turning. By this time Sharon had become more efficient, with the help of her spirit guides, at compressing the time it took to turn negative elementals back into their positive, devic form. Once she had correctly identified who they were, she merely snapped her fingers to accomplish the change. Then we went looking in the park for a place to reattach them—a lovely grove, if they were earth elementals, or a quiet pond, if they were water elementals.

About this time, I discovered that Sharon's soul and one of my souls had shared five lifetimes in the same body together. That explained our extraordinary friendship and close partnership. For more than a year we spoke daily, constantly checking each other's psychic information and dealing with any problems.

One of the most puzzling things about Sharon was the nature of her own soul. By now she had challenged my original reading that she was an Earthling, and we both had difficulty placing her in the categories that we had discovered. The only thing Mark Adam told her was that she was a fallen light being that had been on the planet about 650,000 years. Since my own two souls had been here 11,000 years, and most other people's souls were here for less than 10,000 years, with the exceptions being on the planet no longer than 25,000 years, Sharon's soul seemed unique indeed.

By December of 1990, we were in our own private world of planetary beings, elementals, psychic attacks, and multiple souls. The only authenticating responses we received from the real world were reports of relief when we removed lost souls from people, or ghosts from a home. Although all of these beings were great fun to talk about, the one idea that lacked any real support from historical sources that we knew about at that time, or from other psychics, or even from rumors, was the idea of multiple souls. We desperately sought verification.

Verification came with the extraordinary case of Richa as related in Chapter One. That case was our first successful attempt to perform what I began to call "soul surgery". Sharon, however, did not want it known that she was able to do this work. If such a case were to ever happen again, she wanted me to withhold her name from that person. Puzzled by her reticence, I agreed to that condition. However, considering the miracle she had recently been a player in, and the potential for many more such cases, I really wished to announce it to the world. I started working on a small pamphlet (*Multiple Souls*, c. 1992, Sydney) that would become the precursor to this book.

Chapter 8

The Multiple-Soul Hypothesis

The human body was designed as a single-occupancy dwelling, but occasionally there are comings and goings without a formal change in the leasing agreement. Channeling, for example, that's a temporary sublet, although sometimes these pesky entities move in all their furniture, and you have to call in the Higher State Patrol to evict them. Sometimes the original soul says, "You know what? This is a lousy movie, and I'm not gonna sit through it. I'm leaving." This is known as a "Walk-Out", and if there happens to be a disembodied soul standing outside the theater, he might say, "Hey, do you mind if I use your ticket?" And boom. You have a Walk-In.

—Swami Beyondananda

Even though Sharon and I were constantly working with the idea of multiple souls and finding evidence of their existence in my clients, I was rebuffed whenever I broached the subject with other psychics. They told me that what we were finding were merely different aspects of personality. This atmosphere of denial began to change when Judith Collins, a Sydney spiritual healer, confirmed, after hearing about my perceptions and ideas that, as a clairvoyant, she could see as many as four souls in the bodies of some of her clients. Further confirmation came from a well-known Indian astrologer, affectionately known as Shastriji, who, when asked about multiple souls, said that a two thousand year old tantric text mentioned the phenomenon. The text states that a human body could house up to ten souls. Since my six-souled clients were clearly within that range, this confirmation of my perceptions took some of the responsibility off my shoulders. I had found a link with the past.

Because of the way I discovered my abilities from former lifetimes, I asked many questions about the methods of other psychics once I had arrived in Sydney, where I had an opportunity to meet and work with many of them. I soon learned that at least four of the five senses, sight/clairvoyance, hearing/clairaudience, smell/clairolfactance, and feeling/clairsentience could be extended into psychic skills.

Generally, most psychics are either clairvoyants or clairaudients, possibly because sight and sound are senses emphasized in our culture. I lack these abilities, but have been blessed with the other two, clairsentience and clairolfactance. Of these, only clairsentience has proved to be useful in my work. Since the senses influence each other and since synesthesia becomes active as a result of experiencing subtler levels, that is, deeper levels, of our minds as we evolve spiritually, all faculties in an individual can become psychically active.

The use of feelings and thoughts accompanied by a pendulum, rather than the more common clairvoyant methodologies, has given me access to a unique range of information. With the pendulum, I am able to get a complete, orderly record of a person's past lives. While a clairvoyant would likely see a vivid scene from a person's past in an ancient setting, there would be few visual clues regarding the exact time or place. Since most of us spent much of our past-life history as peasants, and peasant life remained unchanged for millennia, in a visual impression different times and places might be indistinguishable from one another. Three thousand BC in France or 1000 AD in Russia would "look" pretty similar to each other. With the way I ask questions, however, I am given the exact place and time for any particular past life relative to the current one. This means I can determine the very first human life experienced by a particular client, or whether or not the client had any lives in Pakistan in the sixteenth century, for example.

Since the pendulum gives only yes or no answers, one might wonder how the questions can be narrowed down in a reasonable time to arrive at a certain answer. I can only say that, over time, the use of the pendulum sharpens the intuition, which, in turn, helps to form the right questions spontaneously. With this precision in past-life data, I gained access to new avenues for investigation of past-life phenomena. And this, in turn, led me to explore more fully the nature of souls and their origins.

Although our five senses are unable to verify the existence of internal psychological phenomena such as the personality, the ego, or the soul, our culture has assumed the reality of most of these distinct aspects of ourselves for several millennia. In modern times, some of the greatest physicists, such as Albert Einstein and Erwin Schrödinger realized that, at the deepest levels at which physical matter could be explored, we once again meet the world of spirit we carry within. In other words, going as far into physical matter as they could, they met a boundary beyond which we could begin to recognize the deepest aspects of ourselves. Meanwhile, spiritual seers told us that just as our skin separates us from the so-called "external world ", so there is also an inward boundary beyond which we again meet a reality we can share with others, though most of us remain blind to it due to our training from early childhood on, during which what is accepted as "real" constitutes only the so-called outer world.

It seems important to reiterate here that our greatest physicists (I've mentioned only two, but there are others) did not buy into the narrow paradigm being taught as "the scientific worldview" based on strict empiricism. Inspired by physicists such as Einstein and Schrödinger, two neuroscientists broke with that impossibly narrow worldview as well: the Australian, John Carew Eccles and the American, Roger Wolcott Sperry— both winners of the Nobel Prize in neuroscience. These two men were the first in their field to hold that consciousness is not an emergent property of the physical brain, but that, instead, the brain is a receiver and amplifier of the impulses of a non-physical and omnipresent field of pure consciousness. This is a science-based worldview that allows for the knowledge I have been gathering.

Originally, the groundbreaking scientists of the West, including Isaac Newton, Galileo, Copernicus, et al., embodied the best of science and the best of religion in their worldview. The Catholic Church, however, found that their new ideas, such as the Earth encircling the sun, threatened its authority, and began the long division between the two establishments that continues to this day. Psychologists, such as Sigmund Freud, were no help, either. Seeking credibility for new avenues of study, these men avoided topics that were considered to be in the religious domain, such as the study of the soul. This has delayed the scientific exploration of our essence; however, the 'soul' is to human behavior what the 'atom' is to physical behavior.

> The 'soul' is to human behavior what the 'atom' is to physical behavior.

To take the sciences of the mind to the next level, it will be necessary to explore the finer aspects and agendas of our souls. In presenting my hypotheses here, I am sharing unproven impressions that others following me will need to confirm. First of all, we need to re-examine the assumption that our souls are especially attached to our bodies. We imagine that once we are ensouled, a permanent tight union exists that lasts until death. In my findings, the connections between the body and soul can be rather tenuous, especially in the first few months of life. The time in *utero* appears to be a trial period for the soul—an opportunity for it to tune into the lives of its parents. One of my close friends clearly remembers her birth experience and the sudden realization that she had made a huge mistake in picking her parents. Indeed, during her childhood, her parents abused her, with the consequence that, as an adult, she broke all ties with them.

After the birth experience, the soul becomes more attached to the body and cannot easily detach under its own power. It becomes like a fly trapped in a spider web—an easy entry, with no clear exit. Most souls make the best of their situations if they find themselves in a dysfunctional family, for example, or a society in a state of war. During early childhood, most recognize that they are completely dependent upon parental care. When they become teenagers, however, they seize the opportunity to make changes in their situation. They might feel a need to take a break from whatever scenario they are in, and often they will unconsciously guide their person to seek alternate arrangements going forward. These souls are ripe for attracting other souls that were not interested in being a baby yet one more time. In other words, souls may join a living body not just at birth, but also throughout a lifetime, and especially during the teen years.

Thus, we need to reconsider the supposition that one body can only house one soul. This construct has historically soothed us into believing that, in a complex world, some things are nice and simple—one body, one soul. But why, then, are some people so complex that we cannot understand their behavior from one minute to the next? Were we to place a multiple-soul template upon such a complex individual's conduct, his or her behavior would suddenly make much more sense. The moodiness of these individuals, their occupational and relationship oscillations become fathomable. In other words, patterns emerge that are recognizable and recurrent.

One such pattern involves souls that choose to delay their entry into a human body until that body is in its teens. The reason for this particular pattern is the high infant mortality rate in many cultures throughout human history. This mortality rate means that many souls have experienced being born and then living only a year or two, or even less. Some of these souls have not experienced adult life but have plenty of experience of birth and babyhood. As a result, they look for already embodied teenagers and young adults who are facing challenges. These troubled individuals might actually need another soul to share the burdens as well as the joys of their lives.

These souls then make an agreement to join the teenager's birth-soul to form pairs, threesomes, or foursomes inside the body. Just like a group of teenagers enjoying the thrill of cruising in cars, these souls enjoy the thrill of gathering inside bodies and taking turns 'driving' that body. I call these extra souls 'Hitchhikers' or 'Drop-Ins'.

The term 'Drop-In' is similar to the idea of "Walk-In" as first explained by Ruth Montgomery in her book *Strangers Among Us*. A Walk-In is a soul that joins a body whose birth-soul wishes to commit suicide but has the maturity to realize that it need not unduly traumatize loved ones and family members. It thinks, "Why waste a perfectly healthy body when there are many souls who wish to inhabit it?" Therefore, the birth-soul makes an agreement with another soul to enter that body. Walk-Ins usually involve a seriously depressed or suicidal birth-soul that truly wants to leave the body and has the wisdom to protect family and friends from the grief that an untimely, unexpected death would occasion.

So, why don't we know about such internal arrangements? Because even with only a single soul, our internal drama—shared among competing mental constructs such as ego, personality, and soul—is complex beyond our conscious mind's ability to understand the source of a particular thought or symptom. For example, can we always pinpoint the origin of a simple stomachache? We might wonder if the ailment is because of something we ate, or anxiety about an upcoming stressful event, or some malfunctioning of our digestive tract. It could even be referred pain from some other part of our body. It might also be a complaint from our soul. The possibilities are indeed endless.

Since we have so little comprehension of even the workings of a single soul running a body, how could we possibly discover the presence of more than one soul inhabiting our bodies, unless we were previously introduced to the idea and then also had a reliable means of perceiving the presence of multiple souls?

This difficulty in understanding even what is happening in a single-soul situation becomes almost impossible in a multiple-soul scenario, mainly because of the cultural ignorance of the existence of the phenomenon, and also because there is no physical difference in the appearance of a body that is multiple-souled and one that is single-souled. Furthermore, from my consulting experience these past twenty years, it is clear that most souls sharing a body are very compatible with each other, and, working as a team, they smooth over distinctions that might exist between them in order to accomplish shared goals.

The most typical pattern of multiple souls running a body is taking turns in a set sequence of about two years each. The soul in control makes all the major decisions for the individual while the other soul(s) rest and observe. When another soul takes over, it then makes all the decisions. If there are four souls within one body, then they rotate responsibility in a set four-way sequence.

Most agreements among multiple souls occupying the same body resemble four passengers in a car, with each taking turns at driving on a long journey. When one of the resting

[margin handwriting: — can we remove the soul that carries ancestral burden?]

souls takes its turn, the outer circumstances of a person's life might shift somewhat, depending upon that soul's tendencies. When there is a change in 'drivers', that person may seek a career change, or they might shift from feelings of romantic love, to feelings of friendship in a marriage. This latter example illustrates why it is so important to understand the situation of multiple souls. In a typical marriage both partners could easily have two to four souls each, or a possible eight souls between them. The permutations and combinations of such soul-complexes definitely add perplexing new dimensions to the interactions of couples.

Most of the time, multiple souls within one body get along, but the spiritual growth of each soul can result in internal friction or inner calls for a change in direction. This might result in one of the resting souls doing some 'back seat driving'. For example, if three friends are driving across the United States, and, on the way, one suggests detouring to see the Grand Canyon, but the others don't want to, the third passenger may sulk. In a multiple-soul situation, such hidden brooding may result in melancholy, without the conscious mind understanding the real cause of the situation.

Below is another diagram that illustrates the body's relationship to soul(s), as well as to the other more ephemeral attributes.

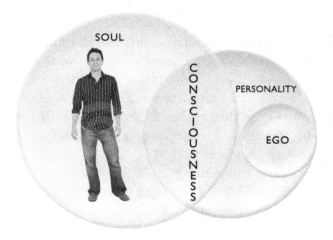

Note that in the diagram, the body is smaller than the soul and yet larger than the personality or the ego. Somehow, ever since my childhood I have thought of the soul as being some small presence inside me. In actuality, the situation may be reversed—in that case, the body is like a kernel inside the soul, firmly attached, but not completely merged.

Soul Origins and Soul Archetypes

Souls appear to have some stable attributes that are expressed throughout their many lifetimes. In my work, the attributes of a soul appear to be related to its spatial origin in the universe. The point of origin is the first feature of its environment when it begins to emerge from Source. But in addition to the attributes of the unique origin of any soul, I have found two more ways of categorizing souls. A soul can be identified by its archetype and by its dimensionality.

When I began this work, I was only aware of two categories—origin and dimensionality. But about fifteen years ago, I realized that while the origin of a soul could not always be determined, my guides were able to classify souls by planetary archetypes according to ancient astrological wisdom. Astrologers sometimes refer to planetary energies as archetypes, a way of naming things that has also entered our language as when a person is called "mercurial", meaning changeable, or "Martian", meaning warlike. While I have found that some souls did originate on Mars, others are merely Martian in nature, i.e., assertive and liking challenges. Nevertheless, the greatest numbers of souls have indeed originated on Mars and Venus. (John Gray must be psychic!)

Astrologers have traditionally assigned a particular archetype to each of the planets. For example, a Neptunian archetype indicates strong intuition and a keen interest in spirituality and music. A Neptunian soul is likely to have these attributes, as well as emanating them. For example, one of John Lennon's two souls was Neptunian.

In addition to the normal planetary archetypes, however, there are a few additional archetypes that sometimes express themselves in souls. Among these are the Chironians, Maldekians, and a huge number of "Moonlets" (my term for souls originating on Earth's moon). I use the following chart for my individual counseling sessions:

Soul Origins

- EARTHLING – normal, likes to form families, raise children
- MOONLET—emotional, sensitive, maternal, intuitive, child-like
- WANDERER - from another star, in service to this planet
- EXTRATERRESTRIAL—newly arrived on this planet
- INTERDIMENSIONAL BEING—from another dimension
- ANGELIC BEING—occasionally angels incarnate in a human body
- BLACK HOLE GUARDIAN—guards the entrance to a black hole, responsible, likes speed
- RAINBOW SPIRIT—bohemian, uses color to heal, feels rootless
- COMETOID BEING—likes speed, fears collision
- MARTIAN—literally from the planet Mars
- VENUSIAN—literally from the planet Venus
- MALDEKIAN—sad, dispossessed, loves or hates technology, especially atomic technology

Soul Archetypes

- SOLAR BEING - CONFIDENT, courageous, loyal, energetic
- MERCURIAN - COMMUNICATIVE, intellectual, changeable
- VENUSIAN - LOVING, sensual, partnership oriented, graceful
- MARTIAN - ACTIVE, assertive, likes a challenge, initiator
- JUPITERIAN - OPTIMISTIC, expansive, happy-go-lucky
- SATURNIAN - WORKAHOLIC, disciplined, moralistic, issues of financial security
- CHIRONIAN - WOUNDED HEALER, sufferer, visionary
- URANIAN - HUMANITARIAN, non conformist, rebel
- NEPTUNIAN - DREAMER, spiritual, musical, intuitive, addictive
- PLUTONIAN - INTENSE, powerful, psychological transformer

Souls can also originate in any number of dimensions at any point in the universe, whether known to us or not. They can come from our moon, or from any moon or comet in our solar system, as well as from any star in the universe or even from inside a black hole.

I have derived dimensionality from the idea that there are many dimensions at any point in space. Rather than thinking of these dimensions spatially, it would be more accurate to think of them in terms of levels or intensities of vibration.

In the working system that I use, the higher the number of a dimension, the more spiritually aware the individual is. The following is a chart outlining the meaning of the various dimensions that I use in decoding an individual's progress in their own spiritual growth, whether they know they are on a spiritual path or not.

Dimensionality

Dimension	Characterized by
Third to Fifth Dimensional Beings	Materialism
Sixth to eighth Dimensional Beings	Half material; half spiritual
Ninth to Eleventh Dimensional Beings	Gurus-in-training
Twelfth to Fifteenth Dimensional Beings	Gurus, masters, spiritual teachers
Sixteenth to Eighteenth Dimensional Beings	Avatars

Soul Origins

According to my guides, Earthling souls make up approximately thirty-five percent of the human population. Earthlings appear to have a shared value system that is readily recognized—a preoccupation with earthly matters, and the tendency to form families and raise children. These are the values that various cultures throughout history have called 'normal'.

The sixty-five percent remaining human souls have extraterrestrial origins and come from some of the planets, our moon, or from distant stars. As I mentioned before, those that cannot be categorized in this way, can be classified by planetary archetypes.

In my work, Chiron appears to be a prominent archetype for souls. Although scientists, and not astrologers, named Chiron, Chironian souls do reflect the ancient myth of Chiron who was half horse, half human. According to this myth, Chiron was immortal but was wounded in a hunting accident. The wound would not heal, forcing Chiron to learn the healing arts. Chironians appear to play the role of a suffering healer.

Esoteric sources claim the former existence of a fifth planet in our solar system called Maldek. According to these sources it disappeared over 700,000 years ago, leaving behind remnants in the form of the asteroid belt between Mars and Jupiter. According to this interpretation, Maldek had a civilization similar to that of Atlantis in that it was technologically advanced, but used its abilities without concern for the planet's stability.

Maldek likely disintegrated due to a nuclear war that so traumatized all Maldekians living at that time that none escaped the knot of fear that resulted. Advanced extraterrestrials eventually came to their assistance to untie this knot, so that they could then remember themselves as conscious beings. This allowed them to heal to the point where they could once more incarnate into either animal or humanoid form.

Many of these Maldekian souls still remain sad, however, and are frightened by the rapidly advancing technologies of our planet. Nevertheless, some deliberately embrace nuclear power, but in an attempt to direct it towards peaceful uses.

Even our nearby moon has been the origin of souls. The Moonlet souls seem to be intuitive and spiritual, much like Neptunian souls, but with a more feminine, nurturing quality. A few years ago I informed a friend of mine that she was a Moonlet. She immediately exclaimed, "When I was a child I was always telling my mother I was from the moon!" Memories of previous origins can be strongest before the soul becomes too inculcated by childhood training in the culture of their birth.

Although intelligent life appears to be absent from our moon and nearby planetary bodies, my work indicates that beings do come from civilizations on these bodies, but in dimensions higher than the third. Though scientists do not agree about the existence of higher dimensions, my Higher Self and my guides find that these other dimensions exist and that we can experience them in earthly incarnations. Though most governmental bodies sending exploratory probes into space have been unwilling to inform the public if they find signs of intelligent life elsewhere in our solar system, this does not mean that such life is absent, either in the third dimension or in other dimensions of the same solar system.

The planetary beings from our solar system mainly come from civilizations in the fifth and sixth dimensions. The reasons why the planetary beings have come here are varied, but most were assigned to this planet to create a better balance and mix of characteristics for this three-dimensional culture. Who assigned them, I do not know. Some of the planetary beings come here of their own free will because they are bored with being ethereal and wish to experience more physicality. When I did a psychic reading for one of my nieces, I received information that she has been on this planet for the past 8,000 years, specifically in order to be a passenger on a space ship leaving our solar system in approximately twenty years from now.

Fourteen percent of human beings have come from distant galaxies, somewhere between seven and ten thousand years ago. They came here as missionaries to help raise the vibration of humanity. They were sent in seed form as souls. My friend, René Breuls, calls these souls "Wanderers", as I said. Just as an oak tree sends out seeds that become little oak trees, Wanderers cannot help being spiritually advanced and of service to humanity, irrespective of how many human lifetimes they have spent on this planet. Their main difficulty with being here is that they have subtle memories of their unisexual form on their home planets. In other words, they came from distant galaxies that lacked male or female sexuality and, thus, the cohabiting practices of this planet are foreign to them. They have adapted to Earth's ways by postponing marriage or readily divorcing, and by lacking enthusiasm as child bearers.

Since they came here on a one-way ticket, they cannot return to their home planet in the same way that an acorn cannot return to the tree that generated it. Once they arrive on this planet, they become enmeshed in karmic webs and find themselves part of the spiritual evolutionary processes that have developed here.

Also on the planet, but in small numbers, are recently arrived extraterrestrials in *Homo sapiens'* bodies. The reasons they are here are also various. Some have been placed here by civilizations that are observing this planet. Others are here with a desire to control this planet. Some are here as healers. Others are here with a strong desire to aid human beings in their struggles to further evolve.

These ET's are invariably unaware of their own extraterrestrial origins, as are many other souls who forget their origins upon entering a body. Nonetheless, they often have strong hints of their off-planet origins indicated by dreams, apocalyptic visions, or feelings of being on a mission. They also have a choice of entering a human body as a Walk-In. And they can enter a human fetus, just as any other soul can. One in a thousand human beings has an extraterrestrial soul operating the body with no other souls involved.

Another type of soul is what I call a Galactic Being. These have usually arrived in a third dimensional spacecraft that landed on the planet thousands of years ago. They are generally humanoids from our galaxy that were able to procreate in the normal way with earthlings. In most cases Galactic Beings came here because their home planet was running low on resources. They could still navigate between stars because of their advanced technology, as in the movie *The Man Who Fell to Earth*. These beings are highly evolved, spiritually and mentally, but somewhat eccentric and secretive.

The last type of soul I have encountered is one I call an Interdimensional being. There are few on the planet, possibly one in two thousand people. I know that two of my clients are Interdimensional beings. One was a successful stockbroker in his thirties whose main complaint in life was that within six months of dating any woman, the woman invariably proposed marriage to him. I explained to him that because he lacked karma, he appeared to be very pure and thus was a highly desirable mate.

Another instance involved a married female client who had never had a psychic reading before. She mentioned that she was quite worried about her marriage because she had become so attached to her two-year old daughter, that she felt that nothing else mattered. Before the child's birth, she'd had a perfectly happy relationship with her spouse, but it now seemed that the child was coming between them. I asked to see a photo of the little girl, and the energy coming through when I touched the image was so powerful that I knew that I was dealing with something extraordinary. I discovered that the little girl had only a single soul, but it was direct from the ninth dimension and had had no previous lives on this planet. I immediately told the woman that in this case her obsession was understandable because her child was practically from the angelic realms, and that holding or touching her would be a meditation in itself. As a balance to this child's energy, I strongly advised my client to learn to meditate, so that she could experience the source of enlightening energies that is independent of any incarnation, including, of course, this special child.

Some Reasons for Sharing a Body

Aside from souls that only want to bypass childhood by joining a body in early adulthood, another scenario involves souls coming from distant stars. Just like new immigrants to a country, they feel uncertain about the rules of planet Earth. They might want to time-share a body in order to take their first tentative steps in learning to live here. They frequently wait to be invited into a body by a birth-soul that is experiencing some distress and therefore in need of help. These immigrant souls want to assist without taking full responsibility for the body. They are therefore willing to come into a body when called.

Janice was a new client in her late thirties. When I talked to my guides, giving them her name and birth date, they told me that the birth-soul was an eleventh dimensional Plutonian. Then I saw that at age twenty-two she had acquired a Moonlet soul, and at age thirty-two she had acquired a Saturnian soul. When I told her this, she commented that at twenty-two she divorced her first husband, and at thirty-two she divorced her second husband. Her situation is a classic case of a birth-soul in distress, crying out for help, with help arriving in the form of additional souls.

Other scenarios involve souls desiring to fulfill a karmic plan to be in a specific place and time. They either pair up or form groups of three or four or, occasionally, even five or six souls, and incarnate in one body. Sometimes such teams form to make a special contribution to humanity. Since each soul contributes separate talents and abilities, the combination often results in a productive team effort. When I look at gifted people psychically, I often find they are multiple-souled. Mozart and Einstein each had four souls, as mentioned, and I believe that Stephen Hawking has six.

Love is another reason to incarnate in one body. There is no surer, tighter marriage than that between two souls in one body. Indeed, such an arrangement may have occurred because of a previous earthly marriage that was especially blissful. These two souls, when they meet again on the astral plane, decide to inhabit one body in their next lifetime. They can then choose to stay fused together for several lifetimes. After about eight lifetimes in various bodies, they may amicably part having truly imbibed enough of each other for a while.

> There is no surer, tighter marriage than that between two souls in one body.

Following such an intense association, when such soul-pairs meet again in separate bodies, especially of opposite sexes, there is an incredibly instantaneous, albeit asexual, attraction, the most overpowering feeling of oneness that either person has experienced. Quite often this absence of sexual attraction can leave them both puzzled. The close proximity of their souls for so many lifetimes allowed for the development of the sweetest emotional and spiritual intimacy, while downplaying feelings of sexuality, possibly because of the incest taboo that exists in almost every culture. Some of my clients find these relationships perplexing because they don't fit any known categories in our culture; that is, they are more intimate than a close friendship, but less compelling than a strong romance. Once I inform my clients of this new, yet-to-be-named category of relating, they are often relieved to have a handle on their puzzling situation.

Caroline came to see me because her partner was distancing

[handwritten marginal note: twin flame]

himself from her. I found Caroline had an eleventh-dimensional Uranian birth-soul and an eleventh-dimensional Venusian drop-in. When I looked at her partner, whom I'll call "James", I found that he had a tenth-dimensional Uranian birth-soul and two drop-in souls, both of the twelfth dimension. The reason that Caroline felt such a strong attachment to James was that her birth-soul and James' Jupiterian drop-in soul had shared bodies in three previous lifetimes. I felt that the relationship would not work out in the current lifetime because Caroline had not felt comfortable sharing bodies with James in those previous lives. This had been the cause of the breakup of that arrangement. On a subconscious level, James resented her for that past-life experience and thus was pulling away.

To sum up, there are innumerable scenarios of souls coming together in one body. These may include the lack of experience among some extraterrestrials in running an earthly body, the decision to join a mission for the exalted purpose of advancing human evolution by forming a committee in a body, the desire to help in a case where another soul is floundering, or a love between souls that transcends all forms of known earthly love—as well as a host of other possibilities as yet undiscovered.

Chapter 9

Soul Surgery—The Early Years

Though most proceed differently, some psychiatrists have attempted to merge an individual's multiple personalities because of the obvious problems of such a condition, and there have been reported instances of success. In a similar way, some individuals who discover that they are multiple-souled are uncomfortable with their condition and want to rid themselves of their extra souls. However, unlike the multiple personality scenarios, the merging of souls appears to be impossible. Alleviating any distress resulting from some perceived disharmony among multiple souls housed in one body cannot be done on a whim; instead, the procedure has to be in tune with reasonable karmic and soul purposes.

Sometimes human free will and choice can be brought to bear on the situation. And when Sharon and I asked spirit guides for help to save Richa (see Chapter One), a partnership between humans and spirit guides achieved the desired results, and we sent one of her two souls to the Light. After the Richa case, when depressed multiple-souled clients came to me, I would ask my spirit guides to relieve clients' problems through the removal of despondent souls, and my guides usually obliged, thus restoring the individual to his or her autonomous state. Nevertheless, given all my experience with multiple souls, I no longer believe that being single-souled is necessarily an ideal condition. Yet when dealing with a depressed soul, the best course is to seek ways of releasing it from a body.

Sometimes, souls in a multi-souled situation have had opportunities to arrange for their own departure. Mostly, however, depressed souls lack the creativity to think of a way to escape from a body and, instead, they usually perform some variation of suicide, whether immediately in an actual suicide, or using a slower way, such as picking up a fatal disease.

Although a person's suicide is a shock to the deceased's loved ones, the existence of a troubled soul in a multi-souled individual helps to explain the many instances in which others fail to foresee that a person is suicidal. How many times have you heard about a suicide in which a relative or neighbor makes the following comments: "Why, I saw him just yesterday, and he seemed so happy. I don't understand how this could have happened." Well, it could have happened because the soul that was quietly depressed in the rear seat has now taken control of the body and can finally act on its suicidal impulses.

Considering the fact that souls usually cohabitate due to a special harmony between or among them, why are there ever any problems? In normal circumstances, souls cohabit in mutual agreement, which results in mutual benefits. Such soul groupings sometimes stay together for up to eight lifetimes. In the first few lifetimes, they are adjusting to each other. Then they might have several lifetimes of shared evolutionary growth. By the end of the eight lifetimes, however, souls may realize there is nothing more to learn from sharing a body. It becomes time for solo rides in the next incarnation.

> Such soul groupings sometimes stay together for up to eight lifetimes.

This realization can occur relatively early in a person's life. The unhappy soul tries to devise some agreement with the others that might include a proviso that it simply ride as a passenger this time. If the other souls concede to this arrangement, then harmony is preserved. If the unhappy soul resents the request or chooses to be mischievous whenever it takes control of the body, then trouble ensues. Thus, for any of various reasons, whether it be depression or suicidal thoughts, it may be beneficial to others in a group to remove a troublemaking soul from the body.

Such a 'soul extraction' is distinct from other, more generally known, processes of soul removal such as exorcism and soul retrieval. These latter procedures refer to the removal from the aura, or from inside the body, of confused or malicious souls that temporarily attach to an individual without the permission of the birth-soul. The Catholic Church uses the term "exorcism" because of its position towards such souls. The Church doesn't give such beings the status of a "soul", preferring instead to call them "demons". Labeling them as demonic, with its negative connotation, makes the banishment of such beings more acceptable to the followers of the Church.

In my experience, exorcism is properly used in situations involving selfish souls that possess the body in opposition to the birth-soul, but it is not appropriate in the case of depressed souls that have been occupying the body with the agreement of the birth-soul.

Soul rescue (also called 'soul retrieval') is quite distinct from exorcism. Spiritualists use the former two terms to indicate souls whose bodies have died and yet are not aware of the fact; such souls thus need to be gently directed to the Light with respectful, nonthreatening guidance. It seems counterintuitive that souls could be unaware of the death of their own bodies, but it happens quite frequently when death is sudden, unexpected, quick, and/or painless.

When I began my psychic work, the ideas of 'soul surgery' or 'soul extraction' and 'soul rescue' or 'retrieval' were incomprehensible to me, but slowly they evolved to become a regular part of my practice. With the collaboration of my guides, I have performed hundreds of such extractions and rescues in the past twenty years.

Early Classic Cases (1990s)

Although I touched upon how I do psychic work in an earlier chapter, here I want to explain the process more fully to prepare you for the case studies that follow.

When I work with a new client, I typically keep a clipboard handy to take notes. Then I say my protective prayer out loud and clear my energy field by putting my right hand on my forehead with my eyes closed, while I place my left hand over my solar plexus. This hand placement automatically balances my body's electrical energy field, so that I become a more perfect instrument for obtaining correct information, and thus also grounding my energies. Then, if the client is present in the room with me, I briefly hold their hand, which helps me to connect to their energy field. And, as noted in Chapter Four, in my right hand I hold my small, egg-shaped stone suspended from a silver chain, thus forming a pendulum. I hold the chain tightly between my thumb and index finger, allowing the attached stone to drop in front of me.

Once I've cleared my energy field and have said the protective prayer, I assume that my pendulum will reflect the highest wisdom available to me at that moment. This could mean that my Higher Self is communicating with me through the pendulum, or that the client's soul(s), or some enlightened guide, is communicating with me through the pendulum, using my nervous system as a reflector.

What I mean by "Higher Self" deserves full discussion, and this will be the subject of Chapter Fourteen. For now, we can think of the Higher Self as the source of all wisdom that is free of ego and self-interest. In some esoteric circles this term has come to mean one's soul, or one's soul co-joined with one's guardian angel, but I use the term in its original Sanskrit sense.

Still, whatever the source of the information coming through the pendulum, it first sifts through my central nervous system, as I swing the pendulum straight back and forth. Therefore the accuracy of the answers provided is dependent on my health and energy levels at the time of the reading.

I start to swing the pendulum firmly back and forth in an arc of about 45 degrees while mentally asking whether the client has any lost souls in the aura. If my pendulum swings counterclockwise, that indicates a 'no' answer. Clockwise indicates a 'yes' answer. This particular yes/no pattern is not universal, but it is the method that I have used since 1987. I then ask my guidance if the client has any elementals in the aura. Then I ask if he or she has any negative thought-forms in the aura. To receive an answer to these three or four questions takes me approximately twenty seconds.

Then I ask how many souls the client has. I always mentally ask "Six or more? Five? Four? Three? Two? One?" Most clients, who, on a subconscious level, are attracted to my energy, have two or three souls. Often people who watch me do this are amazed at how fast and powerfully the pendulum swings in my hand. It looks very much like I am influencing the swing because it is so forceful. But that is not the case. If, for some reason, I am swinging the pendulum towards the right—my 'yes'—but the answer is really a 'no', I will typically feel a drag on the pendulum, and it will noticeably slow down before starting to reverse itself.

Once I determine the number of souls in a person's body, I ask my guidance to identify the origin or archetype of each soul, and what ethereal dimension that soul inhabits. I then ask which is the birth-soul and at what ages the other souls came into the body. After that, I ask each soul individually if it is depressed, if so, for how long its depression has lasted, and if it wants to exit the body with my assistance.

All of this information can be gleaned psychically while the client either sits in front of me, or, if they are at some distance, all I need is their name and birth date. Here is a typical example of how my written notes look, when I have completed the first part of a Soul Reading session:

Soul Reading

Name: Jane Smith   Today's date: 2/22/2000
Birth date: January 1, 1963

Aura Check and Clearing: removed negative thought-forms, 3 angels in the aura, no spirit guides

Souls:

11th dimensional	Wanderer soul	(came in at age 11)
10th dimensional	Angelic Being soul	(came in at age 15)
9th dimensional	Mercurian soul	(birth-soul)

If I don't discover any depression in any of the shared souls, I simply and directly ask the client if they are experiencing depression, as I may have missed something, since I don't consider my readings to be 100% accurate. If they tell me they *are* depressed, then I go ahead with explaining to them the possibility that the depression can be permanently removed right then and there. However, if they are taking antidepressants, then even with the depressed soul's removal, it might take some weeks to feel the effects. In no case do I advise anyone to come off the antidepressants right after any session because these mind-altering drugs have serious side effects and have to be reduced under a medical doctor's care.

Nowadays, when a client gives me permission to remove an unhappy soul from the body, I consult with my guides and take about two or three minutes to stand outside in the fresh air to complete the procedure. In the early days, when Sharon was still my partner, I would call her after the session and ask for her help, and this was the course taken in the case studies that follow. After taking in some fresh air, I would go back to sit next to the client and ask what they feel. They often say they feel 'lighter'.

In what follows, I shall outline some memorable occasions when there were dramatic changes in the client's life.

Takanobu and Yumiko

A Japanese couple came to my home one day for help. Yumiko, the wife, was in Sydney to see one of the best headache specialists in the world. During the entire fifteen years that this couple had lived together, Yumiko was experiencing headaches with no known cause. She was on various drugs and drinking alcohol to try to ease the pain. Because her partner had the financial means, they could afford to seek the best treatment worldwide. By the time we met, however, there had been no breakthroughs in diagnosing the cause of her condition or in alleviating the symptoms.

When I did a reading for the husband alone, the information coming through indicated that there was a past-life basis for the headaches that their current-life connection had triggered. On the surface the relationship was quite harmonious, although the age discrepancy between them—she was fifteen years older—was particularly unusual considering traditional Japanese roles.

When they came for a reading, the complexity of this case

surprised me. I found that in the current life, Takanobu and Yumiko are both single-souled Earthlings. Six hundred years ago, however, these two souls shared an American Indian female body. Their current love was incredibly strong not only because of this experience, but also because of the strange fate they had suffered together in that body. When the Indian woman was forty, she died from being scalped—and it was this that triggered the headaches in this lifetime. Yumiko's soul had experienced the murder directly because she was ruling the body at the time, while Takanobu's soul was a witness in their shared body. As a non-active participant, he did not experience the pain as directly as Yumiko's soul did.

The contact between Takanobu and Yumiko in this lifetime instantly triggered Yumiko's headaches, as memories of that time surfaced in her subconscious. Takanobu, although much younger in the current lifetime, feels great love blended with guilt at what happened, as he helplessly watched his soul mate being murdered long ago. Thus, no matter what the difficulties presented by her current condition, he is fulfilling what he sees as a duty incurred in that earlier shared life.

This past-life scenario, however, was not the only basis for the current malady. After the headaches began, Yumiko started self-medicating with alcohol to dull the pain. This habit had attracted a lost soul to her aura that was addicted to alcohol in its own former life, thus compounding Yumiko's problem.

Once I diagnosed the situation, Sharon stepped in to remove the lost soul. This noticeably changed the intensity of Yumiko's pain to the point at which she knew we could help her. Then, with the help of her guides, Sharon was able to relieve the pain completely for several hours, as she walked with Yumiko to a luncheon we had planned. Sharon's ability amazed Yumiko, but at lunch, when she ordered a beer, Sharon chastised her. We both knew that entity reinvasion could occur at any time if Yumiko weakened her aura by drinking alcohol.

Since this Japanese couple was soon departing for Japan, we tried to impress upon them the need to abstain from alcohol. Abstinence is particularly difficult for an addict, especially in the setting of Japanese culture, which expects adults to drink alcohol. Later, Takanobu wrote that Yumiko was still suffering. Alcohol was the cause. Beyond advising Yumiko to abstain, there was little we could do.

By this time Sharon and I had learned that it was not always possible to correct karmic patterns. Reinvasion by lost souls was always a strong possibility, especially if the habits that led to the initial attachment continued. We urged those consulting with us to abstain from drugs and alcohol if they were susceptible to reinvasion.

Even entering a bar without drinking anything can put one at risk. Being in an atmosphere where alcoholic spirits (pun intended) flourish is dangerous. When I tell people at what time in their life they were invaded, they are surprised. When I would ask, for example: "Were you drinking at a party, or visiting a bar sometime during January," they are amazed, because, invariably, I got it right. They would protest, "I only had two drinks," or "I was with friends and didn't even drink." I then would have to tell them that they are particularly sensitive to reinvasion, and a casual drink at a party, or even being around a group of people drinking, could lead to another episode. It is their choice.

Sharon and I looked for ways to enhance our ability to keep people free of lost souls once they were cleared. I contributed to the effort by empowering solid, sacred geometric shapes with specific intent or thought-forms. The English esoteric school had endowed me with this unusual ability soon after they had taught me how to use a pendulum.

It is well known that pyramids can contain and emit consistent vibrations that, in many cases, preserve living matter and enhance meditation. Few people realize that all common shapes, such as cubes, eggs, and spheres also emit conscious waveforms. These frequencies can prove useful.

Eggs attracted me. Simply holding an empty chicken egg in one hand with eyes closed can be an effective method of inducing a restful meditation, while empowering an egg with designated thought-forms can make it a valuable tool in changing deep-rooted thinking processes. These vibrations seem to work by eliminating stress in a particular part of one's life, thus freeing an individual's consciousness to open up to change.

I had already confirmed these insights when I created what I call an "Astroblock" egg that worked to obstruct negative planetary energies that have been hindering a client for a time. If astrological influences were the cause of even a severe malady, using the Astroblock improved the condition.

Sharon and I used Astroblock eggs to protect individuals we knew who were sensitive to entity reinvasion. All we needed was a photo of the individual upon which we placed the protective egg, leaving it there as a sealer. Sharon would check psychically every so often to verify that the person remained free from reinvasion. Even with this device, however, it was still important that the individual cooperate by abstaining from drugs and alcohol.

The ATM Number

Another unusual case early in my career involved a woman named Penny who came to me for counseling. She complained of feeling constantly fatigued, confused, and directionless. I discovered that her main soul was an Earthling, but for the past three years, she had a ninth-dimensional Wanderer drop-in that was controlling her all day, three times a week. Since the normal multiple-soul pattern is to alternate control of the body for about two years at a time, I felt that Penny's cycle was too disruptive, considering what she was reporting to me about her confusion.

Although it is normal to have three to four guard-attending to a person's needs from birth, it is not always the case that such angels are positive in nature. Indeed, they can sometimes be malevolent. Thus, in Penny's case, one of her three angels was "dark", or had less than good intentions. After determining that Penny had been tired for over three years—the same amount of time that the drop-in had been with her—I felt it would be good to remove both the dark angel and the Wanderer drop-in. She agreed to this.

Sharon and I discussed the case, and by the next morning she had removed both entities from Penny. I had scheduled a second appointment with her two days later to assess the changes. In that second session, Penny had a strange experience to report: "Last night I was trying to take some money out of an ATM machine. Of course, I have my pin number memorized, but when it came time to punch in the number, I couldn't for the life of me remember it. I felt so foolish. I made three attempts to guess the number and failed. Even stranger, when I went home and looked it up in my papers, I didn't recognize it then either!"

My response was: "That's a good indication that we actually removed a soul. I guess you opened that bank account within the last three years?"

Penny said, "Yes. Why?"

"Then the Wanderer soul must have initiated opening the account, as well as memorizing the ATM pin number." We both laughed.

Of course, the main satisfaction came when Penny reported that, even in the last twenty-four hours, she felt so much more energy and less confusion about her life goals. We then examined her soul talents and discovered that she had strong entrepreneurial skills. For the first time in many years, Penny felt in control of her life again.

Monkey on his Back

I met Jane at a New Age Center (which no longer exists) in the eastern suburbs of Sydney. We met during a workshop. We liked each other, and when she found out that I could do past-life readings, she wanted one. A few days later, Jane, who worked as a nurse, sat before me, and we became engrossed in the disposition of her soul. She came from a wealthy Brisbane family in which almost all members were in the medical profession. Her father was a doctor, and her favorite brother, now deceased, had also been a doctor.

It was because of this brother that Jane had wanted a reading. A year earlier, Peter, in the prime of his life, had died of a drug overdose, completely shocking everyone who knew him. Until then, he had led a charmed life; no one had suspected that he had a serious drug addiction.

I introduce this case here to illustrate 'the one that got away'. If Peter were alive today, if he had read this book, and if he had come to me for a consultation—granted a great many "ifs"—I could have helped him. All I could do for Jane was a postmortem assessment of her brother's case.

When I touched his image in a photograph Jane gave me, I soon discovered why Peter was a talented doctor and a well-rounded individual, but I also saw why he'd had a drug problem. Peter had had five souls, four of which were well prepared for his destiny as a doctor and a family man. The fifth soul, however, had had no previous experience as a human being. Instead, its last life experience had been as a monkey. This soul, when its turn came to drive the doctor's body, had felt totally inadequate. The only way it could muddle through the experience of being an accomplished doctor when its turn to "drive" the body came around was to take drugs.

In America, when recreational drug usage was less common than it is nowadays, one would sometimes hear the expression "He has a monkey on his back" referring to a person with a serious drug habit. In Peter's case this was literally true.

The Enemies

Roberto Salvatore had heard that I was a psychic and found me at a café in Kings Cross, in Sydney. He had owned several companies over the years, and when crucial contracts were about to come through, something would often go awry and the contract would fold. Following one such occasion, he came to me with a question regarding another man. He had known "John" as an acquaintance for many years. He thought this person was jinxing his business contracts, as well as his life. Roberto said, "I want to know if this man is attacking me psychically."

Somehow I sensed that I would have felt better if Roberto had never heard of me. In any case, I took his question at face value and said that I would try to discover the answer. First, I did a quick reading on Roberto's souls. He had three souls: a Venusian, a Neptunian, and an Earthling drop-in. Then I did a reading on John and found that he had a power-seeking Extraterrestrial as well as a Galactic Being, and, indeed, the ET was malevolent towards Roberto and capable of harming him, as Roberto had feared.

When I confirmed his fears, Roberto's response was, "I'll have him taken care of."

Though shocked, I dared to pursue this. "What do you mean?"

"You know, I'm a Sicilian. You know what that means."

Yes, indeed. I did some quick thinking, and said, "Oh, I can take care of him," feigning confidence. "I have a friend that can remove the offending soul, and then John won't be a problem at all."

This somehow impressed Roberto, and he thanked me in advance. Of course, I was not sure that Sharon could do it, since the offending soul was one of John's souls who might require some severe persuading, especially if it was happy with the status quo. Still, I had to say something to prevent a possible murder.

My next move required some courage. To reassure Roberto, I had to give him my home phone number. I told him to call me in two days at a specific time in the morning. I frantically called Sharon that evening, but couldn't reach her. The following morning, when Roberto called, I had not yet contacted Sharon. I nervously told him to call back at the same time the following day. He agreed.

Finally, I was able to reach Sharon. That night she reported to me that not only was she able to remove the ET soul, but her guides had also instructed her to take out the Venusian soul from Roberto. Of the five souls between them, only these two had been entangled; thus they both needed to be removed in order to make peace.

By the time Roberto next spoke with me, he had already had a visionary experience involving John: he saw that the latter's power to do harm had been diluted. Upon hearing that we had removed the offending soul, Roberto not only believed me, but also gratefully said, "I would like to give a donation to the two of you. Can I drop it off at the Psychic Association?" I said, "Sure." A heavy weight was lifted from my shoulders.

The Extraterrestrial

In my work, I am often challenged with previously unknown contingencies; however, since many of these cases took place twenty years ago, I have grown accustomed to unusual patterns of soul behavior by now. The following situation, when presented to me, took me by surprise because this person had only one soul, and that soul was problematical for him. At the time, Sharon and I had only been working with multiple-souled people, so removing a soul when there were spares in place seemed unproblematic.

"Terry" looked out of place when he came to me during a "Reincarnation Expo" in a hotel in the western suburbs of Sydney. His expression showed fear, in stark contrast to the festive mood of others attending the holiday expo at this elegant hotel.

I began the reading and discovered that Terry had one soul—a normal enough beginning. Its identity, however, was less comforting. It was a power-seeking Extraterrestrial Walk-In, who must have replaced his birth-soul at some point. This was my first face-to-face encounter with a single-souled Extraterrestrial. Not only was I unprepared for this possibility, I was also somewhat uncomfortable because, of the four types of Extraterrestrials that I knew of—visionary, observer, healer, and power-seeker—sitting in front of me was the last, the most confrontational kind.

"Power-seeker" is a euphemism I created for Extraterrestrials whose aim is to control humanity and/or the planet. And, I had come to believe from the media, as well as from Sharon's limited experiences, that such Extraterrestrials could range on a scale from moderately negative to downright evil. Until meeting Terry, I had only interacted with a few multiple-souled individuals who contained a single and not usually negative Extraterrestrial as part of the package. Terry's situation was a first for me.

For a split second I wondered how to handle the reading, since, as an Extraterrestrial, the person sitting in front of me had had no past lives on the planet, yet he was seeing me for a past-life reading. Terry looked depressed. Somehow, I wanted to do the impossible: remove the Extraterrestrial. But how? I knew that Sharon could dislodge souls, but until now, there was always at least one spare soul remaining in the body. What about this case?

I quickly conducted a silent discussion with my guides. They relayed that I needed to tell the truth. In shock, I began to go on autopilot, assuming that we could change something about the situation, but I knew not what.

The 'Walk-In' phenomenon usually occurs when a soul wishes to exit the body without committing suicide, making an agreement with another soul to replace it. Typically, the exchange requires the person to become unconscious while the process is occurring. Therefore, I had to learn whether or not Terry had experienced severe depression and then whether he had subsequently lost consciousness during some normal daytime activity. These are the prerequisite conditions for a Walk-In to occur and facilitate an ET entering a body.

I also knew that occasionally I do make mistakes in my readings, and considering the information I was about to impart, I wanted to be certain that I was correct. Furthermore, by questioning Terry a bit, I could perhaps acclimate him to the rather alarming information I was about to divulge.

I began by asking: "Were you ever unconscious in your life, such as in a car accident, or illness?"

"Yes," he responded, "Many times, on the football field."

"Did this happen once when you were thirteen?"

"Yes."

Then I probed, "Were you suicidal before that time?"

"Yes, I guess so."

Considering the time constraints on our session, I felt I had questioned him enough. I then said, "You have an Extraterrestrial soul, which entered your body at age thirteen, probably while you were unconscious on a football field."

Being new to the subject of reincarnation, Terry failed to register the implications of what I had just said. He reiterated, "Can you give me a past-life reading? I was really looking forward to a past-life reading."

Although Extraterrestrials sometimes have had a few human lives, most lack any human experience. Terry's Extraterrestrial was one of the latter. I thus had to inform Terry that he had

had no past lives on the planet. I apologized for not being able to do a past-life reading, but said, "I think I can help you anyway."

Looking at his serious, sad face, I quietly risked asking, "Have you been suicidal recently?"

Terry replied, "Yes, three months ago."

"Then maybe you would like to exit this body—you, the Extraterrestrial soul, that is sitting before me? And maybe it would be better if another soul replaced you? I have a friend who can remove unsuitable souls from people, and she may be able to do this for you too. Would you like that?"

Terry looked at me dumbfounded, but softly said, "Yes."

Since the environment was inappropriate for such a discussion and since, moreover, I didn't know whether he could fathom what I was asking, I gave him my phone number, told him to sleep on it, and call me in the morning.

That evening I discussed the situation with Sharon, asking her if she thought it would be possible to induce a different Walk-In to occupy Terry's body. She thought it might be. At least it was worth a try. She felt that she would have time to work on it the following Saturday, and gave me permission to tell Terry.

The next evening Terry called and said, "Go ahead with your plan to change my soul."

"Are you sure that you want to do this?"

"My wife, Karen, and I discussed it quite a bit, and we decided to give it a try." I had not realized that Terry was married.

"Well, my friend has time to work on you this Saturday. You might feel something around your head while she is working. Maybe your hair will stand on end, or you'll notice some static electricity around your body. I don't think it will be too strange. I'll call you on Saturday night to see how you feel."

That Saturday, the first chance I had to talk with Sharon was early evening. "How did it go?" I asked.

"I really didn't do anything," she responded. "All I did was tell my guides, and they did the whole soul exchange for me. I think it went well."

"You mean, they picked a soul to put into Terry's body?"

"Yes, that's what I presume happened," she replied.

"What time did you do it?"

"About twelve-thirty"

I immediately called Terry. I told him that as far as we knew, Sharon had successfully exchanged his soul around noon. "What did you feel like today?" I asked.

"I didn't notice anything special. I didn't feel anything happening around my head. All I felt was extremely tired all day. I just didn't want to do anything."

"Great! That's it!"

Then, over the phone, I did a reading on the nature of the new soul that was now in Terry's body. I found a ninth-dimensional Neptunian soul, four dimensions higher than his previous soul. The Neptunian had been incarnating on the planet for the past eight thousand years and had last manifested seventy years ago in a Chinese male. It had had 670 lives on the planet, which likely meant that it was a rather happy soul, wanting to incarnate so frequently.

Terry was thrilled that his new soul was so spiritually evolved. He was also excited to have past lives. I ended the conversation by advising him to call me any time, but at the very least, I wanted him to phone me every weekend for a while. Terry's soul exchange took place on July 13, 1992, in Campbelltown, Australia.

The following Saturday we spoke again. Terry reported that work was going well. He worked as a grounds keeper for a community college. Usually at work, he had resented being told what to do. For the past week, however, except for one day, nothing seemed to bother him. He noticed that his attitude towards work and towards his supervisor had improved. He also remarked that he had much more energy. When he came home from work, one night he mowed the lawn, on another he raked the leaves. Previously, he would have lacked the strength to do this after work. Terry also reported a new interest in China based on his recent past-life there, and expressed a desire to study the language.

Of course, I was happy to hear all of this, but I was determined to explore if I was possibly dealing with a placebo effect. Since Terry believed that a soul exchange had occurred, he might have been reacting according to this belief. If that were the case, over the next few months he would have been unable to maintain this posture. Only the reality of a major internal change would support continued improvement in his situation. Week after week, though, the same reports came to me from him over the phone. His attitude was positive; everything seemed rosier.

Three months after the soul change, on October 2, 1992, I interviewed Terry and Karen at my Sydney home, recording our conversation. The following are excerpts from that interview:

Ruth: *What did you say to him when he came home that night?* [After the reading at the hotel]

Karen: *I know when he came out of there he was like white, really pale. It took him a while to actually tell me what had gone on. So, sort of spooky, and then we went home, and that was all we talked about. I mean that both of us thought well, you know, it's not going to hurt. I mean Terry was so keen to let it happen and because of the way he had been for quite a while, that any chance of changing his personality and the way he was feeling was worth a go. So, yeah, I went along with it fully; told him it was a good idea.*

Ruth: *What did you notice in the first days of the first week?* [Following the induced Walk-In] *What were your reactions, Karen?*

Karen: *Well, I didn't know what to expect. We have known each other for eight years. He has always been a person who couldn't communicate, would bottle things up to the point of explosion—very angry, very negative. And I guess the first week it was like he was a different person, happier, and could joke around. And I guess he was contented for the first time in a long time. And nothing seemed to bother him at all. Because of the way he'd been, I was just waiting, wondering whether or not it was just a short-term thing.*

But that was the first week, but as the second week went by, and now months down the track, it only seems to have gotten better. The change was definitely noticeable right from the start.

You know in the weeks preceding...the actual Expo, you know the depression and the anger and the sort of lashing out was really there. So in a matter of weeks after the exchange, he really changed. There was a big difference.

Ruth: [to Terry] *Has anyone else noticed this difference in you, either at work or any of your other relatives or friends?*

Terry: *I'm not too sure, but like Karen said, I probably couldn't communicate too well with people, but now I don't find a problem. Now, I always like to have a bit of a chat with people. I'm interested, too, to know where they come from and where they grew up and things like that, where I never was before.*

Karen: *And often, because through his football, we stuck*

in the same group of friends, we never went out of that circle of football friends. I mean that's sort of the whole time we'd been together. Then, you know, just out of the blue, Terry started talking to one of the students a couple of weeks back, a girl at the TAFE where he works, who has no interest in football at all. She's from Ireland and she's spending a lot of time by herself. She wasn't mixing very well at all with the other students. So Terry was talking to her. And they [she and her fiancé] came around.... not long after. For Terry to do something like that—out of that sort of context, of friends—the football people...We would go to the pub and that's the only sort of friends we always had. And for Terry to actually take that step and go up and talk to someone that he didn't know anything about was very out of character. It was something really.

But you know, just in the last couple of months it's probably the best that it's been for years. And I would say that it's got to do with, you know, the soul that Terry had before and the exchange now. I mean it's just incredible, because I lived with him every day. And to see that difference. Sometimes I think, is it the same person? It's just unbelievable. It's not like a [feigned] happiness. I guess he would always [appear] happy even though I knew that he was really down in the dumps. But contentment more now, contented to stay at home, contented to do things, perhaps, that I've always wanted to do, but he wouldn't do it because that's not the in thing to do.

Terry then repeated the idea that he would always go out with his "mates" drinking and sometimes "end up with fights". Then Terry and Karen talked about a night when they went out to a pub for a meal as a couple, with the Irish student and her fiancé.

Terry: *We went out together and had a bit of a meal. And I'd stopped drinking just after I'd seen you and I hadn't had a drink for five months or something like that. So we went out with this other couple, and I had a few beers. Beforehand, I used to get aggressive and violent.*

Karen: *We could never go out as a couple without us either having an argument, and I'd either go home, or he'd go home. And that's the first time probably since we went out about seven or eight years ago.*

Terry: *I used to get angry if I was sitting there having a beer and a drunk would walk past and accidentally stumble into me, or something like that. I'd probably end up in a heap and brawl....But I was there with Karen... and I was having a beer and Karen was having a Tia Maria, I think it was. And this drunk walked past and virtually almost knocked me over and I sort of patted him on the back and said, "You alright, mate?" Whereas before...*

Karen: *That's out of character!* (Laughter)

Terry: *I would have punched him or something. And when we went home, we chatted about it didn't we?*

Karen: *Yeah. And it was amazing.*

Terry: *I had a great night. I even got up. I never used to dance. I had a few dances with Karen, and we went home and had a bit of a chat about it, and I said to Karen this is one of the best nights we have ever had together.*

Karen: *It was amazing.*

Terry: *But I was very proud of me self with that episode with that drunk though, where he wrenched right into me—nearly knocked me off my feet. I sort of said, "You're right there, mate?"*

More than five years later, when I returned to Sydney for a visit in 1998, I contacted Terry and Karen to see how things were going. Their marriage was still strong and Terry was then employed in a new job with a lot more responsibility in a nice suburb at some distance from Sydney. In the interim they had had two children, a boy and a girl, and everything had really worked out well for them.

Just when I thought that my partnership and friendship with Sharon was unbreakable, everything suddenly ended. My wish to go public with the multiple-soul theory clashed with her desire for secrecy, driving a wedge between us.

In 1992, I had begun to write a small booklet about the theory called *Multiple Souls*. When Sharon read the first draft, she felt greatly insulted. She noted that I had not given her credit for multiple souls. This astounded me on two counts, first because she desired to keep herself under the radar, and second, prior to even meeting her, in August of 1990, when I was still in Tokyo before arriving in Australia, I had found that more than one soul could share the same body. It's true, though, that I hadn't used the term "multiple-souls", but I did not consider my use of a rather obvious name for a phenomenon I had noted without Sharon's input to be some sort of infringement of "copyright". I tried to show her the evidence of my previous work on multiple-souled people, but she refused to look at it. We never reconciled.

A year later, while I was mulling over various issues in my life, I decided to consult a famous Sydney psychic to get her opinion on the directions I needed to take next. I brought two photos of significant people in my life, including one of Sharon, to the session, but I said nothing to the clairvoyant about Sharon's association with me. After looking at her photo for several minutes, the clairvoyant said that Sharon and I had known each other in previous lives, and in those lifetimes, Sharon had always been my teacher or mentor. In this lifetime, however, our roles were reversed, and Sharon was having trouble handling her change in status. Wow, did that sound right—especially because I had told the psychic nothing about who she was to me.

Since close friends have always been important to me, I was devastated about losing Sharon's friendship. In addition, I felt crippled by not having her abilities to release lost souls from a human body or to deal with elementals, once I found them. But my guides and angels had a big surprise for me.

Within a few weeks, they responded to my need to acquire gifts similar to Sharon's. They upgraded my soul situation by removing my birth-souls, one at a time, and replacing them with two other souls that were more gifted than my birth-souls had been, so that I could take on the dual role that I now needed with my work. This was all arranged, as I was about to leave Australia under great duress.

The new souls were almost like a consolation prize. I wouldn't be able to stay in the country I loved, but I would have the powers I needed to continue the work I loved. Thus, my new souls were capable of psychically analyzing the energy signature of almost everyone on the planet given just their name, and, with the help of my guides, I was also capable of correcting defects at the soul level.

By late 1992, my guides had carefully instructed me in the unique attributes of human souls, their origins in the universe, their history on this planet, their archetypes, their talents, and their shadows. My guides shared with me their ability to direct lost souls to the Light, to communicate with spirits, and to facilitate the evolution of depressed souls.

Chapter 10

Back to America

By 1992, I really wanted to stay in Australia forever. I had found Sydney safe at almost all hours of the day and night. Such freedom appeared to be only available to me outside of America. It had been over eight years since I had lived in the States, and I was a de facto expatriate ever since I decided life might be more fun in Tokyo than in Boston. And it certainly had been.

Just when I thought I was on track to become a permanent resident in Australia because the New South Wales Department of Education had hired me to teach Japanese history and had sponsored me for immigration, the rug was pulled out from under me. The Australian Department of Immigration insisted that I return to America to reapply for Australian permanent residency from my native country. This was a major setback, which tore me out of my charmed life in Sydney.

I returned to America in February of 1993 and moved in with my elderly father in Pompano Beach, Florida. At 86, Dad was still very active, playing tennis and enjoying many events in his gated retirement community. But after six months of sharing his apartment, he told me that my presence was putting a crimp in his social life! So he "kicked me out". It was really a gentle nudge, but it lessened my considerable guilt about not having spent much time with my elderly parents.

I was still hoping the Australian government would change its collective mind and realize how valuable I would be as a future resident. But eight months and a few thousand dollars later, my application for permanent residency was rejected again. I headed for the West Coast, hoping that something might change, which would then allow me to board the next plane for Sydney. Plus, my most recent Sydney boyfriend reinvigorated my hopes one night, when on the phone, in a drunken stupor, he asked me to marry him! He actually beat me to the proposal, which was awfully psychic of him. Of course, that was too good to be true, so sure enough, when he next called me, and was sober, he withdrew the offer.

When I arrived in the San Francisco Bay Area, I discovered that I couldn't even get a tourist visa from the Australian consulate; perhaps I had been placed on some kind of blacklist. I was mortified and forced to face the fact that I was stuck in America with about three months' savings.

I asked my spirit guides to help me decide where to live, considering that I was without the means to move any great distance. They said "Berkeley", right across the Bay from San Francisco. Since I had been a student most of my life, being close to the University of California at Berkeley made sense. Also, since the town of Berkeley is about ten degrees warmer than San Francisco, I immediately took their advice.

I didn't know anyone in Berkeley, or in San Francisco, for that matter. It was difficult starting over, especially because not only was the whole country in recession, but California's unemployment rate was higher than that of practically any other state. Confirming this gloomy picture, there were aggressive beggars everywhere on the streets.

In a poor section of Berkeley, I found a place to stay, sharing a house with its El Salvadoran male (read 'macho') owner. I hoped to find temporary work soon, and meanwhile, I advertised my psychic abilities in the local paper. I didn't have much choice because, in the steep recession, I couldn't even find secretarial work, which, when I had been unemployed before had been my default job. Five months later, I found part-time work that gave me bare minimum income, which then allowed me to move into my own tiny apartment in a lovely North Berkeley neighborhood.

Once in my own space, I began to feel somewhat normal again. I moved forward in my work as a psychic and past-life reader, even though being psychic in California is like bringing coals to Newcastle. As someone so aptly put it, every other person in California is either a psychic or a massage therapist. I also began writing this book. That was more than twenty years ago. Very soon, I had clients who provided some of the case studies described here. One of those was Andrew Johnson, whom I will discuss next.

Angel Inventor

Of the many unusual clients I have had over the years, some just stand out in my mind as being really important benchmarks of some sort. Andrew Johnson (his real name) was one of those.

Andrew came to me for a soul reading because every time he tried to move forward in life, he was blocked. He suspected a spiritual cause, but couldn't figure out what it was. He was a regular-looking, healthy guy in his mid-forties when he showed up at my door in Berkeley. He looked like the comedian Steve Martin: handsome, but with something askew. I assumed that many people found him odd after hearing his inappropriately loud laughter. He seemed to feel comfortable in front of me, but, at the same time, out-of-place, with an eccentric quality that was hard to define.

I told him my usual protocols for a soul reading: scanning his aura and body, looking for negative thought-forms and entities that I must clear before I could continue my work.

then alerted him to the idea that he might have more than one soul, and that I identify souls by their origin, or their archetype. After determining that Andrew had one soul, I then referred to my soul-type chart to identify the origin of his soul. In Andrew's case the pendulum indicated a 'yes' when my eyes scanned the words 'Angelic Being'. Then I went on to discover the spiritual level of Andrew's soul. As I indicated earlier, I do this through determining the dimensionality of the soul, which indicates to me how advanced each soul is on its evolutionary journey. Andrew had a twelfth-dimensional Angelic soul, which explained his eccentricity to some extent. It is rare to see an angel alone in a human body, as angels are usually too intimidated by the thought of running a human body unassisted. I would say that they have a tendency to be 'flighty', lack a sense of time, and/or space, and are likely to be gullible. Also, in Andrew's case, I was for the first time meeting an angel alone in a male body.

When I asked him the reason he wanted the reading, he said that he was a medical inventor who was being blocked in getting financial and other support for his breakthrough, cancer-fighting inventions. He wanted to know why he was being blocked. At the time, he was supporting himself with odd jobs such as tree trimming and working in a butcher shop—work unrelated to his true gifts.

I discovered two main reasons for the blockage. One was that cosmic and economic forces do not necessarily want a cancer cure discovered at this time, and, more importantly, a cancer cure would remove a major source of income for the existing cancer industry.

The other reason was more specific to Andrew. I found that he had lost his entire, personal angel contingent ten years earlier. Now, why would an angelic being in a human body lose all his pals? The usual reasons one loses angel contingents has to do with flying inter-continentally to places that angels don't want to go, or doing recreational drugs, something they would disapprove, or becoming angry and telling some human "to get out of my space", which the angels take as a command for them to leave as well.

And there is one more circumstance that causes angels to depart: if one is unnecessarily endangering one's "vehicle", or the body. This final reason applied to Andrew. Because on some level we all know who we are, Andrew likely knew on a deep unconscious level that he was an angel, and angels like to fly. When I asked him if he was often flying in planes ten years earlier, when he had lost his angels, he immediately responded with "Yeah, I was skydiving every weekend."

Okay, that explains it! Well, you have lost your entire angel support system, and in order for you to break through the blockages you mentioned, you will need to pray to some archangels in order to get a new angel contingent. Angels are the basis for luck in our lives. Without them we are like free-spinning cogwheels that have lost any connection to the ability to manifest our goals."

I then gave Andrew an energy healing, and he went home and prayed daily for a new team of personal angels. Within a month he had two angels in his aura, which made him very happy. He also took several Seraphim Healing courses from me, and generally felt more contented about where his life was going. He started making plans to get a job that would help him go forward with his medical inventions. He was convinced that he knew how to treat many forms of cancer, and he wanted to test this out in a farm situation. He found collaborators in South America and Africa, and he called me monthly to report on the progress he was making. Then he landed a job with an agricultural hog development laboratory in Yuma, Colorado, and soon I was getting calls from there, as well, telling me what a great job he had found. He worked happily there for over a year, reporting to me regularly and asking me whether this or that collaborator was good for the ultimate medical project he had in mind. He really loved the little town he was living in and had a very nice rental home there. He felt that things were coming together for him, and he was most thankful to me about that, asking me to make sure his angel team was still intact, whenever he called.

Then I traveled overseas for about five months. I believe he called me for a Soul Reading once while I was away. When I returned home, I found that there was a telephone message stored in my messaging service from a company in Yuma, Colorado. I didn't make the connection right away. When I called the name left in the message, I was asked if I knew Andrew Johnson. When I said, "Yes," the woman on the other end said that he was killed in a car crash a few months earlier. They had found my name and number in his address book. I was stunned to realize that such a lovely, innocent man/angel was gone just like that. I also remembered how years before he had endangered his body in skydiving, so I asked the secretary what were the circumstances of the accident. Sure enough, he was a passenger in the car, and he wasn't wearing a seat belt, which would have saved him from bleeding to death before the ambulance came to rescue him, about an hour after the crash.

A Letter from Martina

On a brighter note, about this same time I had a new client from Texas, who called me one day regarding her own issues, and then, because she was satisfied with my reading, she admitted that the real reason she had called was to find somebody who could help her niece.

I asked, "What's wrong with her?" Martina explained that her niece was suffering from sickle cell anemia and was in such serious condition that she might die from it. I had had no idea that this disease could be so virulent. I said that the best way for me to help her would be for me to talk to her niece directly in the hospital, or at least have a live telephone connection to her hospital room, so I could help to adjust the energy there. Martina said that she would try to arrange this as soon as possible. Within a few days I got a call from her. She was in her niece's hospital room. Her niece was semi-conscious, and the hospital had notified all relatives to come and say their goodbyes.

Among the relatives there, Martina spoke English, but at that time, I believed the others spoke only Spanish. I started to work on Martina's niece by going through my usual procedures of removing negativity. Then I told Martina I wished to remove a suicidal soul from her niece's body, one of her multiples. I warned Martina not to tell her relatives anything about the removal of a soul, as I didn't think they would understand the idea of multiple souls because of their stressful situation. I feared that her family would not be open to any discussions of spirits, much less to exorcisms. Martina felt awkward about keeping this secret, but complied. Once my guides had removed that particular depressed soul, there was less reason for Martina's niece to be so ill. Then I tried to boost the girl's immune system by giving her an initiation, using Seraphim Healing energy. Several weeks later I received a report from Martina about what had happened:

"Dear Ruth,

"As you know, my niece was born with sickle cell anemia and since birth she's had many, many hospitalizations. They've put in a valve near her heart that kept getting infected. She never developed. (Her body wasn't growing right, and her brain, or mental faculties remained those of a 6-7 year old). At the time of your healing, she was hospitalized and the doctor told us to gather around her, 'cause she wasn't going make it! I was desperate! I was so

*not ready to let her go! And I cried, and asked the Lord
with as much emotional energy as I could muster, to send
me somebody that would help her release all this disease
- to give my little Lucita a second chance to grow tall
and smart and good... Immediately after falling apart
like this, I went to the 'net to search for a healer, for an
answer, for something to hang on to. I was at the end of
my rope... so desperate... I don't even remember what I
wrote that brought me to your website... I just remember
going through the steps of calling you and being surprised
that you actually answered! I felt that you were so inexpen-
sive for what you offered that I made that appointment
and told my family that I would need to make a phone
call from Lucita's bed. I did not tell them what you were
going to do or what your area of expertise was... I just
told them that you were a healer from Australia and that
I had paid you to help Lucita from a distance! So, here
we were: me, my mother, my sister, Lucita's mother and
father (Lucita's father is my younger brother) gathered
around Lucita to say good bye.*

*"I dialed your number and put Lucita on the phone as
you had instructed. My mother got up and stood at the
end of the bed and held Lucita's feet. As you were praying
for Lucita, my mother seemed to go into a trance and
rocked back and forth with her eyes closed. She said an
angel showed her with pictures and a few words that
Lucita needed help and that my mother should help pull
out the bad spirits from her. As my mother related all
of this, I couldn't help but feel astonished! I had said
nothing, absolutely nothing to my mother regarding your
spirit exorcism! And yet, she knew, she knew the exact
number of bad spirits that needed to leave my niece and
she knew exactly when this was going on! My mother
said the angels told her to pull, but that she didn't quite*

understand "how" to pull or with what part of her body to "pull" with... She said she finally started swaying back and forth and felt as if something came over her... She felt relaxed, and loved... Needless to say, I was speechless, as was everybody in the room... We didn't know what to say or do. Eventually, my brother said that he couldn't understand a word you were saying to him on the phone (he speaks only Spanish!). But, he commented on how professional of you to hire an interpreter to make sure he understood your words... I told him you didn't have anybody else in the room, but this didn't seem to stop him from believing that there was somebody else in the room that was helping you to help him.

"When we finished with Lucita and passed the phone to my sister (who speaks English), and then to my sister-in-law (who does not speak English) and then to my brother, who also doesn't speak English... You prayed for all of them. At this point, we were not talking about angels or demons; we were just accepting your prayers. Afterwards, we hung up. We sat there, silently, until my mother burst out, as loud as she could, that she had seen Angels when you were praying for Lucita. She was so surprised to see these beings and to know that they spoke Spanish! She said the angel told her to hold Lucita's feet real good and to see the spirits that were leaving her - to command those spirits of disease and weakness to leave her body forever. My mom was so emotional: She couldn't believe it! And at the same time, she knew, without a shadow of a doubt, that Lucita was going to get better. Then my sister said that you prayed for her so beautifully. Then my sister-in-law said that "you" were a man that spoke

> **She was so surprised to see these beings and to know that they spoke Spanish**

Spanish! They argued like crazy about this! My sister said that the healer on the phone was female, and she spoke English. My sister-in-law insisted that the healer on the phone was male, and he spoke Spanish. Then my brother piped in and said that the healer on the phone was indeed a female but that she didn't speak English at all, but was completely fluent in Spanish! What? I said. What's going on? The awesome power of the Holy Spirit!! What an awesome way to show us that we were indeed witnessing a miracle. This touched all of us differently. I didn't know if you could take away these demons of disease and of weakness... how great and how wonderful that my mother confirmed that you were doing this.

"Lucita did get better. Within minutes she was sitting up and talking! This is doubly mystifying because Lucita, up to this point, had only communicated to us with one-word comments, and this, only after much urging on our part. This is more or less what she said: I need to sit up, and drink something right away. I feel fine.

"WE WERE AMAZED!!!

"She was talking in whole sentences! She was being direct, speaking of her needs for the first time! Before this, she spent her life just sitting there quietly, not moving much and not doing much. So we didn't know what to do with a talking, assertive 16-year old! The doc came in and said she was doing much better, but that we should still wait and see. I said nothing further because now my sister-in-law piped in and stated that my brother was telling the truth.... that she also heard somebody else in the room talking in Spanish to her, translating your words...

"Put yourself in my shoes. I couldn't hold on to my promise any longer. So, I told them what you had told me not to tell them. You know, about the "extra" spirits assailing

Lucita and about how you didn't want anybody to know you intended to remove them for fear they might stop us from helping my niece. I told my mother I totally believed what she was saying about the angels helping Lucita and about how she somehow participated in getting her well by "pulling". Everybody seemed surprised. How can this have happened? Mysteriously, my niece sat up in bed and told everyone, she felt fine. This is the young 16 year old girl that only hours earlier had flat-lined several times as her heart had swollen bad... she couldn't move, or talk... but wait, the miracles don't stop there...

"By Sunday, she was discharged from the hospital. My mother called me to report that Lucita had called her and that, much to her surprise, Lucita was talking "normally". You see, because she had been so sick, she had not developed like other kids. Her speech was often slurred and unintelligible. She often just pointed to things or muttered some sounds to make others understand her. Now, my mother said, Lucita was talking just like a 16-year-old would. Her voice was firm and intelligible... she expressed all her ideas to perfection, her thoughts, wants and desires... and I was delighted to hear this... I certainly didn't expect this sudden change but was grateful nonetheless.

"I decided to write to let you know all of this and to thank you, thank you, thank you... for helping all of us receive a little bit of the divine and for allowing us to share in His glory.

"As I sat down to write this e-mail I received yet another call from my mother.... I thought her call coinciding with my writing of this email was interesting: all she wanted to do was to talk about Lucita.... My mother said that for her 64th birthday, my brother and his family (including Lucita) took her to a restaurant. My

mother sounded happy, excited and could not contain her thankfulness. She said Lucita had gained weight (for so long Luci looked "dead" if you know what I mean: thin, bony, sad, pale, sick...). My mother said that she could hardly recognize my niece, as she now glows; she looks healthy, a little plumper, and continues to improve on her speech. So you see, the Lord of Heaven has made all of this happen through you, and we are forever in your debt.... so please accept all of our thanks.

Martina. Texas, USA"

Several months after the work we did, Martina reported more progress:

"Today she is doing so great! She continues to talk perfectly; she continues to grow. Her body has developed, and she looks like a regular teenager! She wears make up, goes to dances, wants a boyfriend and is doing a little better in school. In other words, she's part of this world, and we owe it all to your prayers, to the Good Lord that heard us that day. She hasn't been hospitalized since then."

I was as amazed as this family was at the enormous healing that had taken place with Lucita. Nothing as dramatic as this healing had occurred in such a short span of time as what took place in that hospital room on that day. I later sometimes joked about this miracle when talking with friends, saying, "I only need one more miracle to qualify for sainthood in the Catholic Church. Too bad I was born Jewish, as that would automatically disqualify me!"

Chapter 11

Soul-Mates in One Body

Right before the new millennium, the U.S. and Australian governments had agreed to a new visa waiver program, in which one had to only check in with an airline company to acquire the appropriate authority to travel there. So, I checked with United Airlines to see if I would be allowed to travel to Australia, and they said there was no problem. I immediately took the opportunity to return to Sydney and catch up with old friends.

I really felt like kissing the ground at the airport. I was so excited to be back. Sydney had always felt like home, and I believe I had past lives in that area as an aboriginal. I will never forget the time when I walked into a Sydney hotel lobby, and there was a plaque on the wall commemorating that the hotel stood upon land that once belonged to the Eora tribe. As soon as I read the word "Eora", a bolt of energy flooded my body, and I felt these must have been my people. It was great being back.

One of my old Sydney boyfriends, Peter, had beautiful, identical twin daughters, who inherited their father's Dutch/ Indonesian genes, which gave them a slightly exotic, delicate look. I had first met the twins in Sydney when they were fourteen. At that time, Peter had been a single Dad, raising them alone. When, however, they decided to move in with their mother, he continued to dote on them and moved into the same apartment block where their mom lived. By the late nineties, the twins were both working in Tokyo, modeling and helping to support their parents. Since I had also lived in Japan, I felt especially close to them.

When I returned to Sydney in 2000, the twins were both studying at Sydney University. Amanda and Olivia seemed to have it all—beauty, brains, money, and even spiritual understanding. Their father was so proud of them. When I met them again after nine years' absence, they seemed truly blessed, sweet, and innocent. One week later, however, their good luck ran out.

Peter called me that Sunday morning to say that Amanda's boyfriend of five years had been killed two days earlier in a motorcycle crash. Amanda was devastated. Peter wanted me to try to console her. I agreed to see them that afternoon.

Peter and I went to the terrace house in Paddington where Amanda was staying and were greeted at the door by one of Amanda's male friends. The twins were not there. According to their mom, they were out getting food for our lunch, so Peter and I went out looking for some food as well and ran into them. I was still having trouble telling them apart. We all returned to the house and began to eat while Amanda cried occasionally and was consoled by her friends. There were hushed conversations all around me, and I simply completed my meal, so that I would feel ready to handle the counseling session with Amanda. Peter and his ex-wife agreed to my request to counsel Amanda alone, but when we were about to go upstairs, her mother asked if her twin sister could join us in the session, and I consented.

The three of us ascended the stairs to her small, unadorned bedroom. We all sat on her bed, while I attempted to do a proper reading, first on Amanda's soul situation and then on the deceased boyfriend Jason. It turned out that Amanda had two souls, and Jason had three. One of Jason's souls had already gone to the Light, but the other two were hanging around. Amanda wanted to know where they were. I told her the one that loved her most was right here in the room with us. She asked him over and over, "Why did you have to die? Didn't I love you enough?"

It turned out that Amanda felt very guilty because during their five-year relationship, she had been unfaithful on several occasions, and Jason had known it. Amanda now felt that she hadn't shown Jason that she loved him enough, and that this was why he had died. She also felt that she could have prevented his death because she'd had several premonitions of it, and she felt that if she had told Jason, then maybe he wouldn't have died. She kept addressing Jason, pleading with him to come back, and repeating her questions, "Why did you have to die?"

I was extremely conscious of Amanda's youth and knew she had her whole life before her. I knew that every word I spoke was important in the fragile state she was in. And yet I hardly knew the twins, having seen them maybe a total of three times in the nine-year period since they were 14. I had no idea of their values, or their knowledge of the spiritual world, and the karma they were subject to. I felt that this death was karmic, but I didn't want to upset Amanda even more by seeking the basis for the young boy's death. That was to come later. At this point, I wanted to make sure that Amanda didn't pursue any suicidal thoughts because Jason was indeed her ultimate soul mate of this lifetime. This I had discovered pretty quickly, but I was careful in how I worded it for the girls. I needn't have worried: it firmly established my credibility to acknowledge that Jason was Amanda's soul mate.

As the three of us sat on the bed, with Olivia cradling Amanda in her arms, I was racing mentally to find some real words of comfort, that wouldn't just be pap in such a situation. To give me time, I went into my rote explanation of the multiple-soul theory. During this time, I almost never looked at Olivia because I somehow felt that the spirit world was distant to her interests, and that maybe she wouldn't believe what I was telling Amanda, thereby undermining my approach. During the hour or so we sat on the bed, Olivia didn't speak to me directly, but only sought to comfort her sister, whose intermittent sobbing, had taken on the quality of dry heaving.

I wasn't expecting Amanda to be able to process what I was saying about multiple-souls, but then she surprised me by blurting out that if one of Jason's souls was in the room couldn't that soul enter her body so that they could be together forever? With a shock I realized that despite her grief and her sobbing, she had been two steps ahead of me. I went to the open window in order to get some privacy and talk with my guides. They agreed to do it for her. I had no idea of the consequences. Amanda would be my first occasion to add, rather than subtract a soul—although when I thought about it later, I realized that this kind of thing probably happened naturally quite often. I had met a few people in my practice, who carried the soul of a family member that had died either in a car crash or had been a soul-mate going back several lifetimes.

When I told Amanda, that we could, indeed, go ahead with her idea, I could see that this was the first thing since Jason's death that seemed to offer her some comfort. Even more wonderful was that she could actually feel him coming into her body. When we went outside and I was saying goodbye, Amanda asked her father if people could really have more than one soul. Peter answered with a resounding, "Yes!" That seemed to make Amanda feel more comfortable with the process. I told her to call me whenever she wanted.

Amanda's father thanked me deeply, and I returned home. Within a week Amanda asked to see me again and we arranged a meeting. She was a skinny thing to begin with, but now she looked downright anorexic. She was, however, more present and was actually complaining a bit about how it felt to have Jason inside of her. She said that she felt this nervous vibration all the time, and it was interfering with her sleep. When I checked her soul situation I was surprised that rather than finding three souls, I found four. What had happened since the time I last saw Amanda was that Jason's other soul that hadn't gone to the Light, had seen what happened with the first implanted soul and decided to join Amanda too. Amanda was half herself and half Jason. Her body was having trouble dealing with the combination. And Jason wasn't used to being inside a petite, female body. Amanda was beginning to ask questions like "Does this mean that I will never meet anybody else to be with?" She wanted to know if the process could be reversed because she was losing so much sleep with this restless activity going on inside of her. I said it probably could be reversed, but I only agreed to remove one soul at that meeting because I knew that we couldn't do this thing weekly, and I wanted to make sure that she was really fed up with the arrangement before reversing it.

Also at this meeting I asked more questions about Jason's lifestyle to discover the karmic basis for the "accident ". When she had been hysterical, all I had heard about him was that he was a model, too, like the twins. This time, however, I learned that he was dealing drugs, mainly marijuana. He had done occasional modeling to satisfy his parents' curiosity about his expensive lifestyle. Amanda also said that he was a reckless motorcyclist, and that in the year preceding his death, she'd had a dream in which she saw somebody dying from a motorcycle accident, but thought it was one of Jason's friends. She kept meaning to tell Jason about the dream, but something was preventing her. Although our society considers marijuana to be relatively harmless, over the years I have seen it be quite destructive, especially in cases of schizophrenia referred to me for healing. I told Amanda that Jason's drug dealing was a sufficient karmic cause for his young death.

About two weeks later when she saw me again, we agreed that in order for her to move on with her life, and for Jason to be able to have a fresh start too, it was best that they separate. She felt relieved and more settled when we took the other soul out, and sent it with love to the Light.

It was my last day in Australia when the twins drove me to the airport, and we removed this remaining soul. I had strongly counseled Amanda to leave Australia for a while and visit friends overseas, and she was intending to do so. We almost met in Vancouver the following September, but at the last minute her plans changed. I kept hearing about her travels through her father, and Amanda and I once spoke by phone. She seemed a lot better. In the following year she spent time on long meditation retreats, going into silence for as much as a month. I had advised her to explore the spiritual world in the time that she was recovering from this horrific event in her young life, and she had taken my advice. Today she is much stronger, more vibrant and becoming clearer in understanding the true value of time spent in a physical vehicle.

Chapter 12

Richa Reprise

When I returned to Australia in May of 2000, memories of my earlier Sydney experiences flooded back to me. Over the intervening years, I often wondered what had happened to Richa, the little Indian-Australian child who, as a small baby, suffered convulsions until Sharon sent one of her two fighting souls to the Light. All contact had been lost with the key players eight years earlier. Internet searches had proven fruitless. I had been thinking that when I arrived back in Australia, if necessary, I would hire a private detective to find them.

Soon after I landed in Sydney, an acquaintance suggested that I continue my search at the New South Wales State Library. Listed in the current Australian Medical Directory there were quite a few "Dr. Varmas." Only one, however, had an office in Sydney's western suburbs, matching the previous location, and this one also appeared to be the right age, suggested by a 1982 medical degree.

Anxiously, I called the office number. I first asked the secretary if this was the Dr. Varma who had a daughter named Richa. She replied, "Yes." Some relief. Still, there was the strong possibility that he wouldn't want to be reminded of the past. After checking with him, however, the secretary put me through.

Although Dr. Varma only had vague memories of my working on his daughter, he agreed to answer a few questions that evening from home. My phone rang around eight.

"Thanks for calling me back Dr. Varma. I lost your previous phone number, and without knowing your first name, it was a bit difficult to find you. Rajiv's number must have changed, and I can't locate him.

"How is Richa doing? She must be ten years old by now."

"Yes, that is right. She is fine."

"Has she completely recovered from the convulsions?"

"No, she is epileptic. She has had occasional seizures since childhood."

"I am sorry to hear that. I knew that after we worked on her, she was left with some hearing loss, but I wasn't aware that the convulsions had recurred."

"The hearing loss was temporary. There is currently no problem with that. But back then, it took four months before the convulsions came under control. She was very resistant to treatment. There wasn't a day that she didn't convulse."

"What drugs did you try?"

"They tried phenobarbitone, initially, then Valproate for epilepsy and also Tegretol. I can't remember all the drugs that we used."

Then I commented: "At the time, I heard from Rajiv that the drugs weren't working."

"When the dosage was increased, the seizures eventually stopped. In any case, drugs normally take a few weeks to take effect."

"I don't remember Dr. Nayar using the word 'epilepsy.' Was that the diagnosis?"

"The initial diagnosis was epilepsy, and the final diagnosis was epilepsy."

"I thought that when Sharon and I worked on your daughter, the convulsions had ceased. Don't you remember the spiritual work we did?"

"I vaguely remember something—maybe a change in the pattern. Possibly at the time you intervened, the seizures were delayed a few more hours. I do recall something involving Rajiv."

"Oh, we thought that when we worked on Richa, the convulsions had stopped. That's what Rajiv told us."

Dr. Varma replied, "As far as I know, the drugs finally took effect after we kept increasing the dosage."

"I see. By the way, do you know where Rajiv is?

"I think he went back to India for a while. I haven't seen him in about five years."

"Has anyone in your family ever had epilepsy?"

"No. Not in my family, nor my wife's."

"Thank you so much for your time. If I think of some other questions later, may I call again?"

"Yes, certainly."

After we said goodbye, I was left wondering if our spiritual intervention had done anything. I felt an urgent need to speak with Rajiv Nayar. I hoped he would respond to a letter I had sent to his former residence, which was still listed on the national electoral rolls. The Telstra telephone operator, however, could not supply me with a phone number.

Rajiv called the next day. He had finally received my letter. He confirmed that he had an unlisted number, as I had suspected.

After catching up on the past eight years, I told him of my conversation with Dr. Varma that had left me wondering what actually occurred with Richa. Rajiv agreed to be re-interviewed in person a few days later.

When we met, I detailed the discrepancies between Dr. Varma's account of what took place and Rajiv's previous account. I said that Dr. Varma didn't recall much about our spiritual intervention, and felt that drugs had stopped Richa's convulsions.

Rajiv replied, "Well, I personally think that one of the prime reasons that Dr. Varma is feeling the way he is, is that he doesn't have a very strong spiritual understanding. I don't expect a person who is making a living prescribing drugs to say that his daughter got healed by another therapy.

"Although I haven't practiced medicine in Australia, I have practiced for many years in India. Also, I did medical research in India because I wanted to discover new inventions that would help humanity. And that's what drove me to become a doctor."

"But you never used the word 'epilepsy' when we spoke in 1990. Did you hear in the beginning that she was epileptic?"

Rajiv replied: "The reason I didn't mention that possibility is because besides studying medicine I have been a keen spiritual seeker, as you know. In India, very reputed doctors mix these treatments. It is quite common there for a doctor to use medicine along with spiritual healing. So I used the terminology that I felt was appropriate to communicate what was happening. I felt Richa's symptoms were due to something spiritual because of the way Dr. Varma presented his case to me.

"So that's the reason I did not use the word 'epilepsy.' It's nothing more than a term. I'm interested in results, and healing. And I do not care how it happens. Epilepsy, especially petit mal, happens to many children.

"Besides, in my childhood, I had similar episodes, which I haven't told you about. Later I came to know these states are called 'catalepsy,' in which you're half awake and half asleep. I used to see a saint coming out of my body, and buzzing around. It used to cause mild convulsions, or seizure-like symptoms."

This new information amazed me. "How old were you at the time?"

"Well, I think I was four, or five years old. Old enough to know what was happening. And at that time I was misdiagnosed! That's one of the reasons that I later studied this phenomenon of epilepsy. My experiences were not diagnosed correctly, and I was put on medications! And I suffered as a consequence. This is something which I could not tell you.

"Later on, when I studied the occult, I came to know that it is a very common phenomenon. It might have been my astral body, or the soul of another person, or it was something from one of my past lives. I also remember seeing a monk coming out of my body. I do not believe that Dr. Varma has had such experiences. He is schooled in the belief that such seizures can only be called 'epilepsy.' So when I got in touch with you about Richa's convulsions, I did not use the word epilepsy, because it's just a label used by modern medicine."

Since I knew very little about epilepsy, I asked Rajiv if Richa's pattern of convulsing every two hours for four months was typical.

Rajiv responded, "Okay. I would like to give you a medical definition of epilepsy. Epilepsy is divided into petit mal, and grand mal. And petit mal epilepsy happens in younger people most of the time. Again, this is just a phenomenon which is labeled by some Western schools as 'epilepsy'. But even before this label came into existence, this phenomenon was widespread. People used to call it a manifestation of spirit. For example, 2,000 years ago, according to the Bible, Jesus Christ took demons out of people. And society accepts that explanation. So, basically the problem is one school of thought versus another. And now I want to give you a correct definition of epilepsy."

He left the room to find a medical textbook. He returned with a classic textbook written by Harrison called: *Physicians: The Principles of Internal Medicine.*

He started reading from the text: "The epilepsies are a group of disorders, characterized by chronic, recurrent paroxysmal changes in neurological function caused by abnormalities in the electric activity of the brain. They are common neurological disorders estimated to affect between 0.5 and 2 percent of the population, and can occur at any age. Each episode of neurological dysfunction is called a 'seizure'. Seizures may be convulsive when they are accompanied by motor manifestations or may be manifested by other changes in neurological functions. Epilepsy can be acquired as a result of neurological injury or a structural brain lesion and can also occur as a part of many systemic medical diseases. Epilepsy also occurs in an idiopathic...."' He interjected here: "which is a scientific way of saying the cause is not known."

He continued: "In Richa's case I do not know the exact diagnosis, because there are many forms of epilepsy, and I don't know how it was classified. But I assume that it was petit mal, because that's what normally happens in children. And what that is, is that 'The symptoms start in childhood and during an attack the child stops activity.' What that means is that when an attack comes the child just stops all normal activities and just stares. 'He or she may blink, roll up the eyes and fail to respond to commands. Each attack lasts only a matter of seconds, but many hundreds of similar attacks can happen during the day. Occasionally there is a loss of posture and the child may fall.'"

Then I asked, "Did you ever see Richa at this time? Did you ever see her while she was going through this?"

"No, I never saw Richa after this happened. I have only seen Richa healthy, when they used to visit us as family friends. I think her problems caused a lot of sadness, anger and discord in the family. I didn't meet Dr. Varma after that. I got busy, and he probably got busy."

Trying to make sure that I had covered all remaining questions, I mentioned that I was most shocked when Dr. Varma said that Richa's convulsions went from November through March. "I distinctly remember you calling me after we did the soul removal from Richa's body and saying: 'The convulsions had stopped.' That would have been only a month and a half after the convulsions began. So that would have been around New Year's. What was the basis of your saying that the convulsions had stopped?"

"I was just basing my information on my conversations with Dr. Varma. I think that the initial attack was quite acute. He and I are doctors, and we base a lot of our treatment and advice on what one doctor says to another. He was very perplexed and anxious, and that's one of the reasons I got in touch with you. In addition, my mother had recommended that they actually get the blessings of Sai Baba [an Indian saint], who is supposed to have done great miracles on incurable diseases.

"So, when I called you, I'd had some information from Dr. Varma that Richa was better, or that the convulsions had stopped. It's been a long time now; I don't really recall. But I think the attacks had become less acute, and, most likely, I called you to say that.

He continued: "See, from that experience, no matter what physical manifestations took place in Richa, and what drugs were given to her, that became one method he was trying. But I personally have had so many experiences with people having similar episodes and getting better without using medicine, that I'm convinced that Richa's experience was much more than a physical manifestation, or just a breakdown of physiological functions in the brain. And the main question is that even if you read the literature of epilepsy a lot, as I just mentioned, it's *idiopathic*, which means that the cause is not known. It means that there are reasons which science accepts that they do not understand.

"Western medicine was introduced in India with colonialism in the 1850s, but that doesn't mean it was universally accepted overnight. Even a hundred years ago, labeling something as 'epilepsy' was still far from common. Back then, most people would think in terms of spiritual causes in the event of seizures. They would say exactly what you are suggesting: that such symptoms are a manifestation of spirit. And they would use their own traditional medicine, or a spiritual teacher to heal people.

"So if Varma says there was no history of epilepsy in his family, it could mean either that he is hiding the fact, or that it was never diagnosed in Western terms. Simple as that."

I then asked Rajiv about another detail from the past. "After we had agreed that maybe Richa was healed, I remember wanting to know if there were any lasting deleterious effects. I don't know if you remember telling me she might have had a hearing problem afterwards? The other day, I asked Dr. Varma about the child's hearing loss, and he said that it had been temporary, and that now her hearing is fine."

Rajiv replied, "It's well known that the drugs which are given for epilepsy cause side effects, and it's just a matter of checking on which medicine was given, and checking it out with pharmacological data, and you will find that there are many side effects. Her hearing loss could have been a side effect of the medicine she took."

I then recalled our earlier conversation, "I remember you said nine years ago that the drugs weren't working. Is that because they weren't given enough time to work, or that the convulsions were so strong that there was no drug that was really helping? Dr. Varma claims that they had to keep upping the dosage to get the drugs to take effect, but that they finally did, and that's how the seizures eventually stopped in March."

Rajiv replied: "No scientist could say that the seizures stopped solely because of drugs. Of course, drugs were given and you provided spiritual healing, right? So now, Varma chooses to believe that the drugs were effective. Can you put yourself in his position in Western society? A doctor who comes from India, and says 'My daughter was cured by a spiritual healer.'

He'd be called a quack, and people would stop coming to him."

I had to agree, and he went on:

"Right. Concern for his reputation as a Western doctor is one possibility why he said what he did. And the second possibility is, yes, these drugs do help people—in the long run. There are cases of epilepsy in families who do not have any spiritual training, and the patient does get better. So I cannot make any comment, whether it was the drugs that helped her, or it was your treatment. But I can say this much. My experience, with this—my own personal experience—I was misdiagnosed with epilepsy, but it was not epilepsy at all! You understand?

I nodded, "Yes," and he continued:

"Although I didn't have very strong convulsions as a child, I did manifest certain things leading a doctor to call me epileptic, and he put me on drugs, for no reason, as it turned out. And because I was a little child, I could not explain the phenomenon. It was later on when I studied yogic literature and different occult schools that I realized these phenomena are discussed as part of our spiritual teaching.

"So, the real answer might come to you when Richa grows up and she talks, and she tells us what she was experiencing. Because she is a child she cannot yet express what is going on with her. She is ten years old now, but depending on her schooling, and as she becomes mature enough to discuss her experiences, I am pretty sure she will give us some indication of what was really going on with her. Along with her physical symptoms, there certainly must be a subjective component, and, maybe, even a spiritual one."

Having covered all my points of concern, my interview ended, and we continued to chat about our lives in the intervening nine years since we had last met.

These follow-up interviews with the two Indian doctors added a level of complexity to my understanding of Richa's case. Once I returned to America a few months later, I tried to digest what I had learned.

In the meantime, I went to the local public library in Berkeley to do some research on the topic of epilepsy and found a book titled: *The Spirit Catches You and You Fall Down: A Hmong Child, Her American Doctors, and the Collision of Two Cultures.* In the case of this Hmong child, the doctors diagnosed the little girl as having epilepsy and treated her with drugs. They ignored the 'primitive' beliefs of her Southeast Asian culture. To the Hmong people seizures indicate that an evil spirit has stolen the soul. Their remedy was to try to call the soul back into the body.

The American doctors, however, forced their own treatment onto the little girl, even having the child taken away from her parents. In the end the child experienced irreversible brain damage.

This tragedy could have been averted if there had been some form of treatment that integrated Western allopathic medicine with Hmong traditional healing practices. Again, in this example, we see overzealousness on the part of Western medicine's reliance on pharmaceutical drugs to solve complex medical emergencies with a one-size-fits-all mentality, instead of an integrative approach giving the mind, the body and the spirit each it's due respect and healing.

I have received no further updates on Richa's condition. She would now be about twenty-four years old. Of course I was disappointed that the follow-up interviews did not completely vindicate my initial understanding based upon the multiple soul theory. But Dr. Nayar helped me to see that there were different possibilities that could have influenced the way this situation was perceived, and that one's background and professional training could sway that perception in the case of someone like Richa.

If I hadn't had a huge number of successful soul surgery outcomes by the time I had heard Richa's father deny that his daughter was helped by our intervention, I might have come away dejected and concerned about the foundational assumptions Sharon and I had made in this case. Instead, I came away puzzled, but ultimately glad we had made those suppositions, because it resulted in such an enormous potential breakthrough in our understanding of the human condition.

Chapter 13

Enlightenment

The historical literature of the East is filled with docu-
mented cases of people becoming enlightened, a state of
consciousness still little understood in Western cultures. As
a much sought-after condition in some parts of the world,
however, individuals born into such societies sometimes drop
everything from their lives, as did the historical Siddhartha
who, as prince of his kingdom, left his loving wife, family,
and inheritance behind in order to achieve the perfect state of
a living Buddha, or enlightened being.

Maharishi Mahesh Yogi, the master who taught me the
most about enlightenment, informed us that it could come
suddenly or in stages. He said that one would have to complete
one's karma for it to happen permanently, but that we could
get flashes of enlightenment along the way, to give us a taste
of what was in store for us.

With Western clients, I didn't expect my work to generate
such experiences, let alone to draw any enlightened clients to
call me, but when this did happen, I was certainly surprised
and grateful to be somewhat prepared because of my background with meditation. The following is a testimonial from a
woman in the state of Washington who called me in despera-
tion regarding a chronic neck ache. Here are Kelli's own words:

"I do not remember the exact date or if it was before or after my grandmother died, but around the time she did, I started to have episodes with the back of my neck. The sensation is extremely difficult to describe, but here are some words: intense pressure, fullness, swollen, choking, unstable (like my neck could not support my head). I had never experienced anything like it. Nor had I ever encountered anyone who had experienced this sensation. I went to doctor after doctor and healer after healer. Everyone had a theory... "You need a new pillow," "Your MRI shows inflammation," "You need to love yourself more," "It's all in your head. Here's some antidepressants," "You need a chiropractor," "You need to learn to relax, you are too stressed."

These diagnoses were unbearable to hear; no one understood. I was REALLY DYING HERE. This was the most unbearable feeling in the world. I am suffering beyond what I ever imagined possible, and you are telling me to buy a PILLOW? I spent six or so years managing this to varying degrees.

Along with the neck discomfort came a sense of profound and unspeakable doom. I felt cursed. I would tell my kids, who, as they stood there totally helpless as I cried my heart out, that I felt possessed, like there is something in me that I need to get out. I wanted more than anything for someone to understand, to be able to SEE or FEEL how much pain I was in. I was trapped in my own body and the answer to my problem was to get a pillow!? I was brought to my knees time and time again. I found myself begging, pleading, demanding answers.

This journey has been long, but I believe it has come to an end. Right now, I am overwhelmed with gratitude and feel a sense of freedom that only a prisoner released from confinement could feel. There are so many different things that led me to this healing over the past six years. So many, in fact, that I could not remember them all. I have seen over twenty doctors and healers and spent thousands of dollars. I have seen Reiki Masters, medical intuitives, acupuncturists; I had soul retrieval, Reconnective Healers, all types of chiropractors and many more. If you are living in hell, and know there is a way out, but you do not have a map, you just keep going. If I had have given up that hope anywhere along the way, I would have died.

I did not know how to be this person that I am without the pain. I now feel like part of me was kidnapped and just returned home and I have no idea how to interact with myself. I find myself so overwhelmed with gratitude that all I can do is cry. The relief I feel is beyond my ability to describe. I feel this divine love and incredible contentment that it is almost uncomfortable.

I found Ruth on the Internet as I was searching for another healer. When I saw her face on the screen, I felt this warm sense of love and electricity. I knew I had to talk to her. I called and made an appointment for the following day. When I spoke to Ruth on the phone she said she was going to ask her Angel what is going on with my neck. She came back on the line a few minutes later, and asked if I had experienced anything traumatic around the time my neck started to hurt. I said that my Grandmother, who I was very close to, died. I said that I was upset about this, but it was not ultra-traumatic. She had lived a long life and had been suffering a lot the past few years. Ruth then said she was going to put the phone down again. She came back about a minute later and said that when I was 12 years old, a soul attached to my body. This soul was a soul mate of my grandmother's and has been trying to get out of my body to join my Grandma in another future life.

The soul had been trying to find a way out through my neck. Ruth said that souls know how to enter the body but don't know how to get out. She then asked me if she could ask her angel to assist the soul in leaving my body. I was hesitant at first but then said "yes!" please release the soul. Ruth then put the phone down and I felt this breeze on my face and hair. Then there was this horrible taste in my mouth. After that, the neck discomfort was gone. Just gone. I feel like I have been given a second chance at life. I have been trying for so many years to not be a human being with a body because my body suffered so much. Now though, I want to have a body, to be in a body. I no longer have the feeling of wanting to get out, of being trapped."

On the phone Kelli subsequently spoke about the wonder and beauty of all the experiences she had during that week following her release from the neck pain. Her descriptions ticked most of the boxes of what is considered to be classical enlightenment, a concept completely unknown to her. She told me that during that week she felt at one with the world, with her environment. She felt compelling love for everyone, which she hints at when she described the experience as being *"beyond my ability to describe. I feel this divine love, and incredible contentment that it is almost uncomfortable."*

After a week, though, Kelli couldn't maintain this high experience, as she soon felt the pull of her everyday world bringing her down again. She greatly missed the feeling she had that week, but since I knew so little about her, having only spoken with her by phone, all I could tell her at that point was to either learn to meditate, or to take some of my Seraphim Blueprint classes to help her return to such experiences and possibly stabilize them.

This next case study was even more baffling as "the ways of karma are unfathomable," as Maharishi would often say.

Sherry first contacted me by phone from California in

January of 2011. She was a 32-year-old Chinese-American, with a strong upwardly mobile drive. In September of the previous year she had taken some esoteric supplements that go by the label of monatomic metals, such as gold, and other rare earth metals. These were touted to be great for overall brain functioning and health, but in Sherry's case, she felt it had "fried her brain". She reported to me that her short-term memory was completely shot, to the point where she could no longer attend university studies. She also couldn't function in a job, because of severe fatigue, as well as forgetfulness, which was one of the symptoms.

I was quite puzzled by these symptoms, especially because her conversation with me was lucid. She was quite rational as she discussed her condition, and she remembered things I said at the beginning of our half-hour call. Thus, I couldn't understand what was really happening to her. I looked for signs of depression and found that one of her souls was depressed the past seven years. So Sherry agreed to let my guides send that soul to the Light. I also psychically noticed that she had no real physical problems that I could intuitively detect. I only found an allergy to gluten, and told her to try and stay off gluten. I asked her if she had been checked out by the medical profession, and she said she had. I was especially worried about the possibility of a brain tumour, since I know her generation is glued to cell phones.

Then I said that we needed to see what affect my few interventions would have on her symptoms before we tried anything else. I also put in the first healing energy from the Seraphim Blueprint into her body, as that is something I normally do in my private sessions. She seemed to like the energy.

Then a few weeks later she called me again with the same complaints. What we had previously done had made little impact on her situation. She was most concerned that she wasn't "normal" and couldn't function in the workaday world. Again, she spoke lucidly, with no problem in understanding what I was saying in our conversation.

It suddenly occurred to me that from another perspective, she was living in the "Now", very much what many enlightened people have over the millennia tried to achieve from strict spiritual practices. When one lives in the Present, one's perception is bombarded with a huge amount of immediate information coming in to all the five senses that leaves almost no mental real estate left for processing what happened five minutes ago, or what might happen five minutes from now. The Present is glorious, illuminated, and fascinating. Most of us are happy with our occasional "Ah-ha" moments of seeing a beautiful sunset or listening to some exquisite opera singer. But what if all our moments were "Ah-ha" moments? We would seem to ourselves, and others, as very spacey. This would be especially the case, if we clearly remember functioning differently, before a sudden change occurred that resulted in this new state of affairs.

> **It suddenly occurred to me that from another perspective, she was living in the "Now"...**

I immediately got confirmation from my guides that I was on to something in Sherry's case, and I began to take a whole new tack in our conversation. I remembered things that Maharishi had told us about becoming enlightened, and that growing up in Western society, or even a Westernized, Eastern society, prevented us from seeing the signs, or symptoms of enlightenment. Many people had approached him with sad tales of constant insomnia, which they were treating with over-the-counter sleeping pills. When Maharishi checked them out though, he found that they had been lucidly dreaming, --- ere able to function normally during the day; so they

t insomniacs, they just simply didn't recognize one of

the main signs of enlightenment—a constant awareness for twenty-four hours of the day, which meant when they were asleep only part of their brains were unconscious, with the other part of their brains witnessing that unconsciousness, along with a watchful awareness of the body's surroundings too.

Then also, I remember reading a book called *Collision with the Infinite*, by Suzanne Segal, where a Transcendental Meditation instructor of my generation, became suddenly enlightened, and immensely confused by her experiences, where she could no longer identify any "me-ness". She lacked a sense of unity and felt her consciousness expanding outward everywhere with no central point that she could identify with.

I told Sherry about my new theory concerning her condition, and she didn't dismiss it out of hand. I recommended *Collision with the Infinite* for her to read to try and understand her likely new condition, and how perplexing it can be when it first shows up. Because, whenever there is such a major shift accompanied by uncomfortable spaciness, I usually suggest to the client various grounding techniques. I suggested these to her. Thus, I recommended that she eat three warm meals a day, preferably containing some oily foods that would lubricate her nervous system from the inside of her body. I also suggested walking for at least twenty minutes every day, with no specific purpose.

Later, in another session I found out that she was already jogging three times a week for a few miles. I suggested she increase the frequency to help her ground even further. I suggested hot baths—again this is purifying, grounding, and relaxing.

In more recent sessions, as she began to realize what I was saying had some validity, she still complained about not feeling 'normal', and wanting to fit in both with what her parents and society expect of her, as a young, marriageable woman; and these were still her own expectations for herself. I told her that such goals were too narrow considering her advanced spiritual development. Once you become an adult, you cannot revert to childhood. Once you graduate from adulthood, you cannot return to that station either.

Just a week or so after my new understanding of Sherry's situation, one of my most advanced students sent me an e-mail with almost the same expression of the conflict between how an average adult's brain works compared to how an enlightened person's brain works.

Alex wrote:

"When I taught my last Seraphim Blueprint course, I psychically received new information regarding higher consciousness and how the functioning of our brain changes when we access higher levels. It appears that accessing higher levels temporarily leads to significantly increased forgetfulness, and results in a totally changed awareness in daily life. Reprioritizing of sensory input occurs, which means that we assign new importance and priority to some things, and tune out other things that we previously may have considered important. Also sometimes we seem to be in our physical bodies, but at other times we seem to be far away.

With this new information, I was intuitively shown pictures of a computer. From this image, I surmised that all of our brains are like separate computers, with which we experience occasional rare flashes of inspiration. Because of the illusion of personal separateness, in the individual computer metaphor, we are unable to tap into the Source field/God consciousness, so instead we create our own personal data bases by accumulating as much information as possible to store locally in our own brains/computers.

And this accumulation process is also competitive. The

more knowledge one acquires for one's personal database, the more advantages one has for survival, power, manipulation, etc. So when the ego discovers that storing information IS power, the choice is consciously or unconsciously made to close available access to group consciousness and/or Source. Thus, using average consciousness, each individual accumulates as much knowledge and information as possible, but then tries to protect it by not sharing it freely. This mindset further blocks the channels to Source and the all-encompassing shared consciousness.

But now, shifting into higher consciousness has become for some an involuntary process. Recently more people are connecting to Source, in a new process of networking that in the computer analogy is like connecting to the Main Frame/Cloud. This goes beyond just a combined storage of data – it actually opens the possibility of shared access of all data available AND a process of shared thinking. It's like a giant brain that we can all access. Its computing capability is exponentially greater than the sum of an individual's contribution.

At some future point, more people will become aware of this new option of accessing and processing information. And they will be able to tap into it, or involuntarily experience it episodically. This will lead to compatibility issues. It will not be possible to permanently run both from our local PC (ordinary consciousness) and from the Main Frame (enlightenment)."

Alex's vision of this conflict between ordinary consciousness and enlightenment is quite original and his sending his thoughts to me synchronized with my deliberations about Sherry and her 'problem' of not feeling 'normal'. But it highlights a serious issue regarding how knowledge is currently maintained and stored in modern societies. It is imperative that we begin to include knowledge of enlightened states in Western education, so that people who are bordering on enlightenment don't go to the local pharmacy with complaints about insomnia. We need to stop drugging our youth, who might be experiencing states of wonder that are completely outside of ordinary consciousness.

With the increasing vibration of the planet, more and more enlightened people will spontaneously appear in societies around the world. We need to be prepared for this changeover, and be able to protect the health and well-being of all those who are transitioning, as well as those who have yet to catch up.

Chapter 14

A Fellow Psychic

"Which one of us is me?"

New Yorker Magazine 2014

It has now been many years that I have been a psychic and a healer, and, just as people do in any other profession, I have grown and changed. My understanding now is far deeper than it was when I began. My current perspective first took form in a long discussion I had with a fellow psychic in San Francisco. I think it's because we were both psychics that that particular conversation had a great impact on the direction that my thinking took over the ensuing years. It tied together many different strands of my previous knowledge and understanding and helped to give me a unified foundation upon which I now base my work.

I recorded the conversation, and what follows is an edited version of that recording. Most of the changes reflect the difference between spoken and written English. Others were made for the sake of clarity—after all, in a piece of writing, the living context of two conscious beings in tune with one another and with the moment would be missing. I've done what I can to recreate this context, and I present this conversation because it contains, in seed form, the philosophical and theoretical basis of my work.

As I had begun to gain a local and national reputation as a psychic, I also had a regular job at a local psychic fair. This is where I met Donna, a fellow psychic. Since we were both readers at these same events, we hardly had time to get to know each other. We merely acknowledged each other's presence, knowing we really connected. Donna was a short, extremely attractive, and vivacious blonde in her early forties.

One Saturday, we were both working at a psychic fair in San Francisco. It was a slow morning, and since we were without clients when Donna walked past my table, she said: "You know, I really think I need a reading from you." A few minutes later she sat down in front of me, and we began.

Her main question concerned the source of some deep sadness that seemed to reside around her heart. She had no idea why it was there, but it was causing her considerable unhappiness and had been doing so for a long time. She said that she was happily married and really couldn't pinpoint a cause.

When I did the soul reading, I discovered that Donna had three souls, a Venusian, a Jupiterian, and a Saturnian Moonlet, the last one being her birth-soul. At the same time, I discovered that this birth-soul was the sad, depressed one, and that it wanted to leave her body. I told Donna.

Because the idea of "removing" her birth-soul sounded like a drastic measure to her, she wanted to discuss these things with her husband. She asked if they could come to my home for a private reading the next day. I agreed and gave her my *Multiple Souls* pamphlet to prepare her.

Around noon the following day, the two of them came for a two-hour reading. I discovered that at the pre-birth stage, Donna's birth-soul had only intended to be with her until age thirty-two. Now she was forty-one, and that soul was anxious to leave.

After some opening remarks, Donna asked some incisive and important questions:

Donna: Who's the 'I' that makes these decisions? Who's the 'I' that you are talking about, and what do people mean when they talk about the Higher Self? And who is it that is going to be making decisions today?

Ruth: That's three or four questions—all of them spot on, and the one to start with is the one about the "Higher Self", but in order to answer that question, or any of the others, we first need to have a little philosophical background.

Donna: Well, I hope it won't take too long; we could be here all day and get nowhere.

Ruth: Sure. I will keep it short and simple: You can either believe that the world is made of matter and that consciousness is a by-product of electro-chemical brain activity. Or you can believe that pure consciousness, empty but knowing itself, created all that is in the universe. That's it; you choose.

Donna: That's a no-brainer. I don't really have a lot of education, but as a psychic, I think spirit worlds are real and don't depend on somebody's brain waves for their existence. Besides, if consciousness is nothing but a by-product of brain activity, then there couldn't be any life after death. No, the brain is not a generator of consciousness; it's more like a receiver.

Ruth: Yes, all that is absolutely right. So then, what people call the "Higher Self" is just that: pure and infinite intelligence. In Vedic culture it's called "Brahman" or "Atman". Ultimately, they're the same.

Donna: Why two names?

Ruth: It has a bunch of names not just two, and I don't even know them all. Just like Eskimos have fifteen words for 'snow', the Vedas, the ancient wisdom of India, have numerous words for 'consciousness'. Whatever name you call a particular state of consciousness depends on the general context of the discussion and the state of consciousness of the people doing the discussing.

For instance, if you're talking about the meaningful and intelligent silence that informs all languages, then you don't call it Brahman or Atman, you call it "Para", but, ultimately, no matter which name you use, Para, Brahman, or Atman, they all refer to that unified field of empty intelligence that knows itself and that underlies and gives birth to this or any other universe. Brahman has more of a sense of "God-ness" to it, while "Atman" has more of a sense of what the New Age calls the "Higher Self".

So when the discussion is about who I think I am or who any human being really is, then we use the word Atman—the Higher Self, which is ultimately identical with the divine intelligence that created everything.

Donna: But wait a minute. I get the Higher Self; so exactly what is the...well, the lower self? And where do souls come in? Plus, I don't experience myself as infinite emptiness. None of this answers the other question I had, "Who actually makes decisions?"

Ruth: You're asking all the right questions and you've come up with some of the right answers. We all know what you've just called the "lower self ". That's the individual self that experiences itself as separate from the outside world. We can just call it the "small self" for now. Some people use the word "ego" for the small self, but that gets confused with Freudian terms and Western psychology. As for infinite emptiness, some experience that in meditation. And others can suddenly, spontaneously, have that experience, even if they don't meditate. But it's not necessary to experience this on a conscious level in order to evolve into higher states of consciousness. Repeated transcendence is all that is necessary.

Donna: Gee, now you are opening another can of worms. What do you mean by "higher states of consciousness"? I've heard about them of course, but I wonder if they're really real.

Ruth: Yes. Winston Churchill once said, "We are all worms, but I do believe I am a glow worm."

But seriously, if you know where to look, you can find discussion of higher states of consciousness in writings from every culture. Thinking and writing about higher states of consciousness have been marginalized in both Western and modern Eastern cultures.

Donna: I asked about the Higher Self, and I like your definition. But I'm still not clear about what it would feel like to actually experience it.

Ruth: That would depend on your state of consciousness. Maharishi Mahesh Yogi, my main guru said, "Knowledge is different in different states of consciousness." That includes knowledge of the Higher Self, and so we'll get to that. What else?

Donna: Decisions. Who is actually making decisions? My Higher Self? Or my lower self?

Ruth: Well, to the extent that this question can be answered at all....

Donna: What do you mean?

Ruth: How that question is answered depends on what state of consciousness we're talking about, so we have to get those out of the way, but remember the deepest principle we started with? Pure consciousness, or pure intelligence, empty but knowing itself, created this and any other universe. At the level of universe creation, no human being can answer this question about who really makes decisions. And then, even at the human level, they say that karma is unfathomable even to the enlightened sage, and so, obviously, any decision we make is all mixed up with our karma. But at more practical levels there can be some answers, and we'll get to those. So, do you want to know about different states of consciousness?

Donna: And before I forget, why don't you start off by defining what you mean by consciousness and by "states". "States of consciousness".

Ruth: When I say "states" I don't mean California or Texas.

Donna's husband, who'd been listening quietly, broke in and said, "Well, I'd say Texas and California have different states of consciousness."

We laughed, and I said, " Yes, you're right. We really could talk about different cultures exhibiting different states of collective consciousness, but let's not go there.

"So I think we all understand what I mean by 'states'. Water has three states: liquid, vapor, and ice—the same "stuff" in different states. And most humans are aware of three states of consciousness: waking, dreaming, and deep sleep.

Donna: I'd call the last one "unconsciousness".

Ruth: Yes, you can call it that, but you're not dead in that state, and it has its own characteristic brainwave pattern that's distinct from brainwave patterns in the dream state and different again in the waking state. Those three states of consciousness were the only ones Western science acknowledged. But then, in the sixties, Maharishi kept insisting that there is a fourth state of consciousness that is achieved in meditation. Finally, Western science caught up with him in the seventies and eighties, and, using biofeedback technology, recorded a distinct brainwave pattern for that state. There is no Western term for it, and "fourth state" is a clumsy term, so we'll just use the Sanskrit term for it: *Samadhi*.

Donna: So, nobody in Western culture experienced that state and talked about it until Maharishi came to the West?

Ruth: Oh, they did, but they were discounted as "mystics"; most people, especially scientists and intellectuals, didn't take them seriously. When I was in grad school in the seventies, "mysticism" was practically a dirty word.

Donna: Who are some of these Western mystics?

Ruth: There's one text that's especially well known, though we don't know the author's name. That text calls the fourth state of consciousness, or *Samadhi*, "the cloud of unknowing". But if you research it, I doubt you'll find anything that connects this "cloud" with *Samadhi*. Even so, I have no doubt that this connection will be made. It's a pretty good name for the emptiness of the fourth state, though Maharishi would not have used that name even if he'd known about it. As a marketing genius, he used terms like "Cosmic Consciousness" and "God Consciousness".

Donna: True. I wouldn't pay some guru for showing me how to enter some cloud, especially a cloud of unknowing. Why haven't you written something about all this?

Ruth: [laughing] I had it up to here with academic writing when I was working on my Ph.D. I was demonstrating that some of the early American Shakers achieved at least *Samadhi*, which accounts for both their tolerance and their creativity, which made them culturally very different from the Puritans who were rigid and not very creative at all.

Donna: Cute.

Ruth: I didn't mean that they were Puritans, just that their academic belief structures were as rigid as the Puritan belief structure. When I was working on my doctorate, the fashionable theory at that time was called "deconstruction", and nobody was allowed to think outside that paradigm. They wanted me to "deconstruct" the Shakers and show that their culture was nothing but empty talk.

Donna: So tell me who were some Western mystics?

Ruth: St. John of the Cross, St. Teresa of Avila, and St. Augustine, to name a few.

Donna: Never heard of them except maybe St. Augustine.

Ruth: Like I said, the Western tradition has marginalized this kind of thing, keeping such knowledge secret behind monastery walls. There have always been a few scholars on the fringes who've written about mysticism, but in the absence of a well-known technology for achieving stable higher states of consciousness, these people have seriously misinterpreted a few things.

Donna: Like what, for instance?

Ruth: Well, they've argued back and forth about which kind of many temporary experiences are characteristic of the "greatest" mystics. In other words, they judged what Maharishi would have called "flashes" of different higher states consciousness, including *Samadhi*, but were unaware that these "flashes" could be stabilized and that there was a natural progression of these states.

Donna: But didn't you say that there were Westerners who understood states of consciousness?

Ruth: Yes I did. But there's a big difference between the mystics and the academic scholars who study them. The academics most often have zero experience that could be called "mystical", and if they did, they wouldn't admit it—at least not until they had tenure. They take their lack of experience to mean that they are more "objective" than the mystics themselves in assessing various experiences.

Donna: Well, *that's* stupid. That's like a geographer, who's never been to Wisconsin, telling everyone he's more objective about his knowledge of Wisconsin than somebody who actually lives there.

Ruth: That's a good way of putting it. I think you're getting a sense of why I didn't stay in the academic world. But let's get back to your questions. If you meditate regularly, using a technique that's designed for this, then a fifth state of consciousness develops. What happens is that the brain learns to sustain *Samadhi* right along with the waking state of consciousness. And when you can sustain *Samadhi* even during dreamless deep sleep, then that's called the fifth state, or, according to Maharishi, Cosmic Consciousness. Anyway, whatever you call it, Maharishi called it the first stage of enlightenment. He said you start witnessing your own ignorance.

Donna: And like I said earlier, I've never had that experience of pure emptiness. Does that mean I'll never get enlightened?

Ruth: If you meditate, and lead a clean lifestyle, you'll get there. The research says that everyone experiences *Samadhi* in correct meditation, but often it's for only a couple of seconds. People have to maintain that state for at least three seconds before the conscious mind realizes that a break in ordinary waking consciousness has occurred. But however brief *Samadhi* is, it usually happens many times during a typical meditation, and you get the accumulated benefits over the years that you practice. Some people never consciously have a clear experience of *Samadhi*, but if they meditate regularly, they'll get to the next state. I'm pretty sure you've had momentary experiences of the fifth state of consciousness.

Donna: Really? How can you be so sure?

Ruth: Have you ever been alone in your house and the silence gets so thick you can almost touch it?

Donna: Yes...

Ruth: Or you're alone somewhere and you just have to look over your shoulder because it really feels like someone is watching you?

Donna: For sure!

Ruth: Well, that's because your Higher Self really is watching you. That's why that fifth state of consciousness is sometimes called "witnessing"—you become a witness of your life as if it were a movie you're watching. Sometimes it feels the other way around, and you feel like you're all of space, and you're watching this small person that's doing something routine like peeling potatoes. Runners experience this state—they call it "being in the zone". Musicians experience that. So do poets when they feel that they're not the ones writing their own poems; instead, they're just recording what the "muses" tell them.

Donna: Yes, I've had experiences like that. Does that mean I'm already enlightened?

Ruth: It's hard to know, but it's called "enlightenment" when you consistently witness deep sleep.

Donna: That sounds like a contradiction. You're unconscious when you're in deep sleep and yet you're "witnessing" it?

Ruth: Yes, it does sound impossible until you experience it. Let me explain. It sounds impossible to have two streams of awareness at the same time, but in recent years it has been referred to in the West as "lucid dreaming"; as it appears that more and more people are having this experience. Even whales, with their big brains sleep with part of their brains awake so they won't drown, and they remember to surface every twenty minutes or so to breathe.

Donna: I see. If that's possible, then being dead asleep and watching yourself being dead asleep is really possible. Weird.

Ruth: If you know some really old people, you'll hear some of them describe something that sounds like witnessing deep sleep. Maybe you've had the experience of witnessing the dream state. You're dreaming, and you're watching the dream, knowing it's just a dream.

Donna: Yes! I have had that experience.

Ruth: Well, when witnessing becomes constant through all the other states of consciousness, waking, dreaming, and deep sleep, then that's the first stage of what can be called enlightenment. And for some Buddhist sects, that's it. But for Maharishi, and many others besides him, that's only the first stage. These days it gets more complicated, and people spin a lot of words about how intellectual understanding is not realization—no argument there, but then they go on with realization is not liberation, and liberation is not enlightenment; nor does the hairsplitting stop there.

Donna: I get it. A kind of one-upmanship.

Ruth: [laughing] Yes, there are even chat groups, where nothing but that kind of one-upmanship goes on, with everybody describing infinite amounts of evidence that whatever state they're in is the highest state and everybody else is lower.

Donna: What kind of evidence could they come up with?

Ruth: Well, it is true that while you're developing Cosmic Consciousness—or the fifth state or whatever you want to call it—you are also gaining access to deeper and more "subtle" states of the mind than the regular waking state normally has access to, so people describe endless experiences or abilities, always sure that their experience or ability means they've achieved a higher state of consciousness than anyone else in the group. I'm sure you have so-called "subtle" experiences. You're a psychic, so I am sure you know what I'm talking about. Everyone has special abilities that are dormant and that would wake up and become useful through regular practice of meditation.

Donna: Is this where your multiple souls come in?

Ruth: Yes, but let that go for a minute and let's finish up with states of consciousness. After 'witnessing' or the fifth state of consciousness is established, development of the sixth state goes into high gear. Like I said, you can have what's called "flashes" of higher states of consciousness—they're brief and fleeting. And like I told you earlier, this has confused the Western tradition of mysticism, especially because meditation techniques were allowed only behind the walls and locked doors of monasteries. So people outside those walls naturally had all kinds of mystical or "subtle" experiences, but no way to make any sense of them. Maharishi called the sixth state of consciousness "God Consciousness ". In that state, all that you see is radiating divine light. Not only that, you start noticing that plants and animals and stones, especially crystals, are all made of consciousness and *are* conscious. That state is called "God-Consciousness" because you see the divine nature of things everywhere you look.

The next state, the seventh state of consciousness, is called "Unity". Nothing in that state changes from the previous state, except that you don't just see divinity everywhere you look, you *are* that divinity yourself. Meister Eckhart, a German mystic said of this state, "The knower and the known are one. Simple people imagine that they should see God as if he stood over there and they are here. This is not so, God and I, we are one in knowledge." And he also said, "The eye with which I see God is the same eye with which God sees me." That's Unity. Some people go on from there to Brahman consciousness and beyond.

So, now, skipping a few centuries, another Western mystic who thought in terms of those same states of consciousness was the poet-artist-philosopher William Blake. He called what the Vedic literature refers to as "ignorance"—"single vision". The Vedic literature sometimes calls it "the unity of ignorance", which kind of makes sense in terms of what Blake calls "single vision".

Donna: Let me guess, does Blake call Cosmic Consciousness, "double vision"?

Ruth: You're close. He calls it "two-fold vision".

Donna: So then, "three-fold vision" would be God Consciousness and "four-fold vision" would be Unity?

Ruth: You got it.

The Seven States of Consciousness
According to Maharishi Mahesh Yogi

State	Attributes of Body	Attributes of the Mind
1 Deep Sleep	Deeply resting	Dreamless/no thoughts
2 The Dream State	Slightly active sleep	Slightly active mentally
3 Waking	Active	Active
4 Transcendental Consciousness	Deeply resting	Highly alert, experiencing pure consciousness without an object
5 Cosmic Consciousness	Waking, dreaming and sleeping in normal activity	Transcending 24 hours a day, 7 days a week, in co-existence with the first three states.
6 God Consciousness	Waking, dreaming and sleeping	Refined perception able to experience the finest aspects of creation
7 Unity Consciousness	Waking, dreaming and sleeping	Experience of the unity of oneself with all objects. The gap between the knower and the known is bridged.

Donna: Wouldn't the world be a lot more peaceful if people meditated and developed higher states of consciousness?

Ruth: Yes. But throughout history powerful groups, like the Church, prevented the general population from achieving higher states of consciousness mainly so they could maintain control. On a more every day and modern level, I have a friend who got herself fired from a lectureship at a Catholic college because the nuns thought that the very idea of Unity Consciousness didn't maintain the proper and polite distance between God and his "creatures".

Donna: [laughing] Oh, you're kidding?"

Ruth: No. Anyway, that takes care of states of consciousness, and now we can get around to souls.

Donna: Ruth, how have you managed to know all this?

Ruth: Maharishi really was a great teacher and a great writer. I've never seen any accounts of Vedic literature better than his. He was also very clear in his own writing and speaking. He had the rare skill of being profound without being complicated.

But, I still don't like what has happened to the "TM Movement". It has a rigidity and dogma that maybe was his fault and maybe not. He himself was aware that all was not perfect within the movement. My take on the situation is that he was a visionary, but his followers who created the organization were just bureaucrats.

Donna: That makes sense.

Ruth: Another remarkable thing about Maharishi was that he was comfortable in a number of different disciplines. There are videos of him talking to well-known experts in a number of fields and impressing them with the depth of his understanding. He had a university degree in physics, but my good friend, who is a literary expert, tells me that his commentary on Vedic literature is not only profound as commentary, but is also brilliant literary criticism, theory, and scholarship. His influence on Western culture is huge and deep, though it may never be acknowledged. There have been a lot of other Indian gurus, some great and some ludicrous, but none of them so far have been as clear and as comprehensive as Maharishi in their different disciplines.

Donna: Did he teach you about Western mysticism and the stuff you told me about Blake and the other mystics?

Ruth: No, he didn't. But after I learned all I could from him, I saw the Western tradition with different eyes. While working on my doctoral dissertation in history, I really paid attention and researched historical evidence.

And then, living in Fairfield, Iowa, certainly was educational—that town probably has more Ph.D.'s per capita than any other Mid-Western town of ten thousand. One of my closest friends there is a Blake scholar.

Donna: I see—is that the friend you keep mentioning?

Ruth: Yes. And while I'm thinking about her, there's something really important to keep in mind: no matter what states of consciousness you get to, you never lose individuality. Maharishi made that point too, and it's too often overlooked. A lot of New Age teachers somehow think that you lose the small self when you realize the big Self and that we're just basically all alike

> No matter what states of consciousness you get to, you never lose individuality.

in the big Self. True, but at the same time, you lose nothing. On the contrary, your individuality becomes stronger, more established, and more creative. When we get to talking about souls, you'll see that souls are distinct individuals with their own characteristics.

Donna: Well, can we move on now to multiple souls and the decision I have to make? You know, once I understand that there's a big Self and a small self, it's really hard to see where there's room for souls in the system that you described. And you also said that although the question of who makes decisions can't really be answered, on a practical level there are answers.

Ruth: Souls make decisions. But first we have to talk about where souls fit into what you're calling a "system", because that seems important to me. Remember that we kind of touched on the fact that, as you develop higher states of consciousness, you also become aware of deeper and more "subtle" inner experiences. You see levels of awareness within yourself that you couldn't access before. I know that's got to be true of you because you're a psychic. Anyway, we could think of the mind as having layers. Even Western psychology thinks in those terms. Westerners do use such terms as "the subconscious mind" and "the collective unconscious".

Donna: Aren't there layers in physics too? I mean, atoms exist at a deeper level than molecules, and subatomic particles are deeper than atoms.

Ruth: Yes, that's exactly right. And deeper than subatomic particles is what's sometimes called "the Unified Field". There is no consensus on that state, but some physicists, including Nobel Prize Laureates

Ilya Prigogine and Eugene Wigner hold that the "Unified Field" is pure consciousness.

Donna: Well, if that is so, then is the Unified Field what you call Brahman or Atman?

Ruth: Absolutely. Wigner used to be one of the physicists whom people quoted when they wanted to argue against the idea that the Unified Field and Brahman are the same, but what's not so well known is that he changed his mind before he died. Now, the reason I'm bringing up layers is to answer your earlier question about where souls "fit into the system". Vedic literature thinks in terms of four layers.

Donna: And the deepest layer is Brahman, which some Western physicists are beginning to identify as "the Unified Field". Yes, this is starting to make some sense.

Ruth: Moving from that deepest layer outward, the next layer is called *Pashyanti*. That's the layer we have to explore to answer the question you asked about where souls fit into the scheme of things. We're going to skip that level or layer for now. The next layer outward is *Madhyama*. We all know that layer. It includes thoughts, memories, mental images, and so on. It's what we think of as our private inner world—which is not so private to a psychic. One Western term that could apply would be "the stream of consciousness". Moving outward from there the next level is called *Vaikhari*. That's the level of expressed speech and writing. That's language in the physical world. It exists as sounds and as symbols on paper.

The important thing is that I wanted to give you a context so you could visualize those four layers. If

ᵉ from the physical level, speech or writing
ⁱ) inward, then the next level is *Madhyama*,
inking level". Inward from there is *Pashyanti*,
......ᴜ under that is the Unified field (Brahman or the
Big Self). I'm going over this ground again just so you
understand that the layer we're calling *Pashyanti* is
deeper than the conscious mind, but it is not as deep
as pure consciousness. We can come up with Western
names for all those layers or levels, except *Pashyanti*.

Donna: That's really interesting. Are you sure about
that? What about "the subconscious mind" or the
"collective unconscious"?

Ruth: Good question. Really good question. The
reason we can't use either of those terms is that neither
one of them covers the "whole ground". Both those
terms restrict consciousness to the human mind. Some
linguists have said that languages have a "deep structure"
and that in the deep structure all languages are one.
That would be a *Pashyanti* level perception. Not all
linguists can see it. And, predictably, those who can't
see it accuse those who can of just spinning academic
jargon to impress everybody. And then, those who can
see it accuse those who can't of ignorance—which is
what it is.

Donna: So then, why can't we call it "the Deep
Structure"?

Ruth: Because "Deep Structure" refers only to language,
but *Pashyanti* includes a lot more. It includes souls and
sacred geometry and the subtlest manifestations of
physical nature in terms of energy waves where name
and form are one.

Donna: Wait a minute, let me get this straight. Name

and form are one, does that mean what I think it means?

Ruth: [laughing] Well, I can't answer that till you tell me what you think it means.

Donna: Well, if name and form are the same, a guy named "Baker" should be a baker. If you say "kitty cat", a real kitty cat should just show up because you've pronounced the words.

Ruth: Yes, and if you're clear enough and not clouded with stress and all kinds of self-contradictory desires, that's how it would work. It's the origin of the worldwide custom called prayer in most places. The Vedic literature uses the term *Pashyanti* when the context of discussion is language. The word literally means "the Visionary". It's a "psychic" realm by definition. And when the discussion is about the energy waves and sacred geometry in that same visionary field, then that literature uses the term *Laya Vijnana*.

Levels of Speech/Creation

Levels of Creation	Meaning	Western Concept
Vaikhari	Ordinary Speech/writing	The spoken and written word
Madhayama	Mental speech, thoughts, memories, mental images	Unspoken words
Pashyanti (Laya Vijnana)	Strong intention & desire. Also the 'Deep Structure' of Language, and likely where souls & sacred geometry can be located. Field where name and form are one.	No equivalent Western term
Para/ Brahman	Subtle pure conscious expression, available to those who are highly evolved, received from the Cosmic Creator	Possibly the "Unified Field"

Donna: These names are going to be hard to remember.

Ruth: There won't be any need to remember them. I'm just giving you the "system where souls fit in". I wanted to make sure you understood that it's not just me talking through my hat. Mystical traditions see those "realms" that are deeper than ordinary thinking. And it's not just mystics. Some linguists get glimpses of this—and also some mathematicians. Anyone going deep enough in their own field will get glimpses. My whole point is that Sacred Geometry and souls are real, and all cultures get glimpses of that reality.

Donna: So, where does that leave us with big Self, small self, souls, and especially multiple souls? And if we're thinking about removing one of my souls, who will make that decision?

Ruth: OK. First off, I have to tell you that "small self" is just a kind of convenient verbal shorthand. Maharishi didn't speak in terms of souls, and I'm pretty sure that the reason was that there were already too many foreign ideas he was importing to the West without getting mixed up with souls, never mind multiple souls. But with the term *"Pashyanti"* he certainly prepared the ground for souls. We could say that souls are patterns of *Pashyanti* energy.

> **We could say that souls are patterns of Pashyanti energy.**

Donna: I thought *Pashyanti* was a level of language.

Ruth: It is. But remember that *Pashyanti* is identical with *Laya Vijnana*. It's about context. If we use *Pashyanti*, we're talking about *Laya Vijnana*, we're talking about souls and about the field where name and form are one. What I've called "Sacred Geometry" is part of this field. Remember that at this level of reality everything is imbued with meaning and life.

Donna: Have you refined what you learned from Maharishi?

Ruth: Possibly, but I don't expect that TM teachers would agree with me because for them Maharishi's teachings are frozen in time.

Donna: Yes, I understand the loving blindness of devotees.

Ruth: Yeah, that is a good way of putting it. So what I have learned through my work is that whichever soul is currently in control of the body is the so-called small self and it is the one making decisions. So the ninth-dimensional Jupiterian soul is 'you' right now. The situation is like changing channels on a television set. In your case, your personal TV has three channels. Currently you are in the Jupiterian phase. So the person looking through your eyes, talking to me, thinking and emoting is the Jupiterian, which is *not* the birth-soul.

As the name clearly says, your birth-soul has been with you from birth. It's the one that probably chose to follow one of your parents into this lifetime. Most often, the birth-soul comes in because it has past lives with either the mother or the father.

The usual concerns people have about removing a birth-soul are the following: you might feel less connected with one of your parents, or they might feel less connected to you. All of your close friends and relatives from this lifetime, the people that you are emotionally closest to from your childhood or teenage years, might experience a slight shift in how they feel towards you, and you might register a slight shift in how you feel towards them. After all, the sadness of your birth-soul casts a kind of shadow on all your experience. That sadness and its shadow would go. But your memory would stay intact.

So if your birth-soul were to leave today, it would not be a huge change in who you are, or who you feel you are. There would be no loss of memory when that birth-soul leaves. Memory is a kind of holographic matrix in which each point contains the whole. That matrix interweaves the experience of all three of your souls as you experience this lifetime, and you would remember all of your childhood when the birth-soul was the "channel" you were tuned into. I used to think that maybe you would lose some of your soul talents, but have found that this is not really the case because of the structure of that holographic matrix that constitutes what you call your memories.

The only thing that would go would be the sadness. There might also be some shift in how you feel about your husband and your relatives.

Donna: I don't have any relatives.

Ruth: Those would be my concerns, if somebody were to tell me that I was going to lose my birth-soul. Frankly, I think that I have already lost my birth-souls. I think I was born with two souls, but both exited my body in the last four years, not through my own will, or conscious choice, but through their own desire, or possibly with the arrangement of my spirit guides. Now, I believe I'm a Walk-In.

Donna: What exactly do you mean when you say "my will"?

Ruth: Okay, I had two birth-souls. So you could think of that situation as a car and its driver and passengers. So "my will" was usually the will of whichever of my souls was driving the car (or the body) at that moment. But it could also happen that the soul in the back seat could say something like, "Please make a left turn here. There's an especially wonderful view down that way." But in the case of the two souls leaving my body—that was not through my conscious will, not through my conscious thinking state. Instead, it happened while I was asleep, or traveling internationally. In any case, I was too preoccupied with other events in my life. It wasn't a conscious choice.

Donna: If they are gone, who is your "I"?

Ruth: Yes, they're gone. Now I'm a two-souled Walk-In. I've got two different souls. "I" is whichever one is driving. My spirit guides, or my Higher Self, pulled a fast one on me.

You know, it's very hard to look at your own stuff. It's very hard for me to know who I am now. My current mentor doesn't even believe in multiple souls. So I can't ask him to look and see if I am a Walk-In. He doesn't have a clear sense in this area. He is teaching me different skills and abilities. In any case, what I am seeing is that every twenty months or so, my "I" shifts to another soul. But I don't think there is a permanent "I" on the level of souls. The big Self, the Atman, on the other hand, is permanent and immortal. And the matrix of memories is not affected by these shifts, and it's this that gives you a sense of continuity.

Donna: I understand that.

Ruth: We did the car metaphor. But we could also say that the body is like a tape recorder. We put in a new tape. The tape recorder is the same. The body is the same. There's a new tape in there now. Tomorrow I will put in a different tape. It will think of itself as 'I'.

Donna: Right. That's a very good analogy. Okay, I got it.

Ruth: [laughing] It's a new analogy.

Donna: Thank you. But it's not the first time I have heard this.

Ruth: Really?

Donna: Well, when I was going to school to study my own psychic abilities, we talked about that. We talked about more than one soul being able to run a body. We talked about one soul running many different bodies.

Ruth: You might be able to think of the Higher Self in terms of running many different bodies.

Donna: But I have, actually, in my work helped a soul exit a body, because the compatibility between the several souls in that body was gone.

Ruth: So, you induced a Walk-In then?

Donna: Well, no. It was like two or three souls sharing one body, but the soul's entrance was not for good reasons. It was more like a possession. So, it was causing this person a lot of problems. I remember the first time it happened, it was by accident, which is how it happened to you, when you say you no longer have any birth-souls in your body, and you didn't consciously arrange for such a change.

Ruth: Donna, you are referring to a dark soul that entered the body without the permission of the residential souls. And you're describing the removal of a dark soul, in a unique situation. It was a multiple-soul phenomenon that could be quite common. Other spiritual teachers over the eons probably removed problematic souls, just as you did, but didn't make the distinction between such souls hanging out in the aura, or such souls being long-term residents in the body. This is the difference between what the New Age community refers to as 'lost souls ', but they have yet to pick up on the multiple-soul phenomenon.

Donna: I was doing bodywork [massage therapy], and I kept feeling this other person, so I asked this presence to remove itself. And when it did, her body shook. It was quite dramatic. And I saw this being leave. It was a male energy. And that soul's agenda was really not in alignment with the other soul that originally inhabited the body, and it changed her life. She cried. You know, it was really quite dramatic.

I reassured Donna a bit more in preparation for the removal of her birth-soul. I told her again that her memory would stay intact, even if the soul were removed, and that she wouldn't lose any of her abilities, especially not her psychic gifts, which were the basis of her livelihood. Then she wanted to know how the removal of her birth-soul would affect her health. Again, I saw only improvement, if she made the change. She asked about any possible effect on her marriage. I told her there might be some subtle changes, but actually it could make her marriage stronger.

Ruth: Do you have more questions? Or, should I just go ahead and remove the soul?

Donna: Are you going to do it right now?

Ruth: I don't know. Probably. [We laughed loudly].

Donna: Let me have a cigarette first [giggling].

Ruth: Sometimes when I do a major soul change with the person talking right on the phone, they don't believe that it's happened. So I don't know in your case. [Considering how sensitive Donna was, I was being extra careful in the timing of the soul change, wanting to make sure that we picked the right time for her to have the best possible experience.] That's why I'm going to ask when I can do it.

Donna: [quietly] I want to do it now.

Ruth: I think it will be okay. You want to take a little break? You can take a break. Let me just ask, when we are going to do this. [Checked with my pendulum] Yes, we are doing it now, but you take a break.

Donna: We're doing it now! Ruthie!

Ruth: Yes, I feel strong energy coming through.

Donna: [Returning from the verandah] It feels like you've done it! Already!

Ruth: You should know better than I do.

Donna: How are you feeling?

Ruth: I'm feeling fine.

Donna: Good. I could feel it leave! Yes, the area around my heart has an empty feeling, but also feels lighter. Ruthie, what is this?! What did you do?!

> **Ruthie, what is this?! What did you do?!**

Follow-up Session with Donna, ten days later:

Ruth: So, you left here last time with one less soul.

Donna: [laughs out-loud] Well, the way I've experienced it, something definitely left. I remember telling you that it always felt like somebody crying inside of me, and every time I tried to get in touch with that, I couldn't release that feeling. Actually it felt like another being inside of me. It was very depressing, and I would be sad for no reason. I always tried to put a finger on why I was sad, but there was really nothing going on in my life to make me sad. And having done the work that I have done, I really didn't think I was dealing with childhood stuff, because I know the difference between feeling the effects of that stuff and feeling another presence in my body. Since you sent that unhappy soul to the Light, I am seeing things differently, and there is a whole restructuring going on. Now, when I get angry or upset, I feel that somebody is silently instructing me and saying, "That's old; you don't have to react like that anymore."

I feel calmer. Tom [her husband] said to me last night, "You're a lot calmer than you used to be." But the thing I don't understand, and the thing that I would put to you is this: *who* is the 'me' that's having the experience? And who is doing the instruction? Something happened in me, definitely. But there is a part of me that's here, that's always been here. On the other hand, there's something that's behaving differently. I don't know who the hell I'm talking to inside of me. It's like my body had been programmed with automatic responses to situations, which have now changed. I can feel it. I don't know what to call it. It's new instructions. It's a gentle reminder, "Now wait a minute, you don't have to do that anymore." Now, in my work, I always taught being in the present moment, and being in choice, in each moment. You always have a choice as to how you want to react to any situation. So, that has always been in my awareness, but what I'm feeling now is not coming from the "me" I've always known.

Ruth: If you hear some new gentle instructions inside,

you know as a psychic that when we removed your birth-soul, that was facilitated by my guides and angels. So hearing someone new within yourself might mean that you have acquired a new spirit guide in the process. Another possibility is that your small self has become more integrated and aligned with your big Self, or the wisest part of who you really are. That wise part is now giving you gentle instructions to smooth out your path from this point on.

Donna: There's a clarity that I have now that I didn't have before. There's less fear. There's a more comfortable feeling that I have in my body.

Ruth: Hmm. I'm just asking if that is due to the soul change, or due to the [angelic healing] energy that I put in your body. [I had initiated her into the healing system I co-founded with a Seraph, which is now called Seraphim Blueprint, but I didn't have a name for it at that time].

Then, swinging the pendulum, I said, "You know what I'm getting: it's the soul change and not the angelic energy. That was one thing. You know I did correct the energy, you know those energy shifts that I put in, but that's separate from this, I think. That's just an energy shift. It's not a personality, or soul, or anything. So this is a soul change and the voice you hear in your head, my guides tell me it's your Higher Self."

Donna: But whose Higher Self?

Ruth: Yours, Honey!

Donna: If there are two souls there, and I know you gave me several good analogies explaining this… There is something that's constant, that's always been there. That's the way it feels.

Ruth: That constant thing is your Higher Self.

Donna: But see, this is the thing. My personality; who's the person? Who is Donna Owen? That's my whole thing.

Ruth: Let's say we all know who Marilyn Monroe is. By the way, she had three souls. Let's say somebody creates a play about Marilyn Monroe. And you become an actress. And you try out for the part and you do very well. So you are now on stage as Marilyn Monroe. You learn all of her habits, her behavior, her reactions, her way of looking, you know, all that. In that same way, the drop-in souls that have come into your body, they know how Donna Owen looks and acts.

Donna: But again, who is Donna Owen?

Ruth: Well, Donna Owen has a personal history now of forty-one years.

Donna: Whose history?

Ruth: It's a fused history. It's a fused history of three souls. It's a committee inside you. If you are driving a car—let's say it's an old Ford—it has all its quirks, and it's ways of behaving. And there are now two passengers left in this car, each taking turns driving the car. The car doesn't change the way it drives down the road. The car doesn't change the way it gives off smoke in the back. The car doesn't change the way it interacts with the environment. The driver changes, and this change doesn't affect the movement of the car, how fast the car goes, how hot the engine gets.

Donna: That doesn't work for me. One driver can be really racy, slams on the accelerator all the time.

Ruth: Right, so those are changes that can happen.

Like how fast the car is going to run. I mean given the same amount of gasoline, the car is only going to run so far.

Donna: Right.

Ruth: Some people can wear out the car faster than others, the same car. Some people can treat it gently and so the car lives longer. Some people can turn corners and make the car do handstands, and some people are scared to do that.

Donna: Yes. Because I feel like my...

Ruth: So looking through the windows of the car, the windows are the eyes of you. Your body is the car. Looking through the eyes of the car didn't change at all, because I didn't change the soul that was driving when you came to me. So you wouldn't have noticed a huge shift, as if I took out the soul that was running your body. And also, remember that the soul that was the birth-soul [which my guides removed] had control of your body for the first fifteen years of your life, the formative years, all by itself. So it formed Donna Owen, or whoever you were up to the age of fifteen. And then you got these add-ons, or drop-ins. Then the Donna Owen who you were initially said, "This is how Donna Owen works. She likes this, and she doesn't like that. Be careful with Donna Owen." Then they come in and watch initially how Donna Owen works, and then they take over, and they try and imitate Donna Owen. They come as close in accord with the birth-soul as they can, given their own directions, their own needs, and their own sensitivity, their own past-life history and environment. And then you are also growing up and taking on new abilities as an adult in our society, at the same time that you are integrating two other souls. So the process gets confused. So like in Japan, to use another analogy, they have puppets, almost life-size: One man runs the arm, one man runs the left arm, and one man runs the head. So there are three people running this one body.

Donna: Right. It's incredible.

Ruth: So you have souls learning how Donna Owen previously worked, also learning how Donna Owen just had her first sexual experience. And hey, [they say] it's my turn now. You are becoming an adult. The new souls get an ability to add on their own little tricks.

Donna: I feel so much has happened in the past two weeks. I still feel that I need a lot of time alone.

Ruth: You can still do psychic readings now? Do you feel any abilities lost, or gone, that you needed? That was a big question.

Donna: No, I don't think so.

Ruth: Is there anything else?

Donna: I feel like I am looking at my spiritual work here on this planet very differently. Very differently. I feel that I am still formulating the way. Now I feel I deserve more.

Ruth: You mean since the soul change?

Donna: All this has just happened. The biggest thing is that even crying is gone.

Ruth: It's really gone?

Donna: It's really gone. It's an empty peaceful place now. I can feel more connected to my body. It was right here. You know how many years I have been going through this pain. I would sit and do this meditation, and talk to my guides. And when I look, it's gone. It's an empty peaceful place now. I mean that's a miracle to me. To have that sense of depression gone. I feel like I belong now. That's an incredible feeling. I never had that feeling, of feeling safe, and feeling like I belong. All this has happened in two weeks. It seems like so long since I've seen you. When I came to you I had no expectations at all. I had none. I didn't have a list of what I would like. Maybe I am just trying really hard to believe this is true. When I came to you, I had no expectations. I have been just noticing these shifts. I have never gone for two weeks of my life without having that feeling of sadness. I said to Tom the other night, "I am going to just choose to be happy about it. And Tom said, "That's great!" There is a lot of fear gone. That's a miracle.

Even now, years later, I still agree: it was a miracle. A miracle and a mystery. The theory and the philosophy that comes through in my conversation with Donna certainly makes sense to me, and they represent time-honored traditions found in all cultures thousands of years back. But every time I am part of a healing, all I can really say is that it's truly a miracle.

Some Words About Self-Diagnosis

Just recently one of my students, who after having read a draft of this book, wondered if bouts of depression that she had experienced over her lifetime were due to a soul that was trapped in her own body. Being psychic, she asked her guides if this was the case, and they replied 'yes'. So she requested that if they could, would they please remove the depressed soul. They accommodated her request. She immediately noticed that she felt lighter. And the word 'lighter' is generally how clients describe the feeling after they have had a soul removed.

This, however, brought up something I had failed to include in this book—which was some kind of advice to the individual who has similar concerns for their own situation. In general, I don't feel that most people are able to hold a conversation with their guides or angels. Even those who can interact with them, may still lack confidence in their making such an important diagnosis. Furthermore, most such entities are not experienced in this process and may be experimenting with this notion for the first time.

My student suggested that granting that I feel I cannot replicate myself that readily in this work, that maybe I could hold workshops to help people through the process. Although that thought never occurred to me before, it may be the right time to consider it.

I truly wanted to bring this book out sooner, but being blessed with several unusual abilities, I had trouble choosing where to put my attention. Until recently, my focus has been on developing the Seraphim Blueprint system (SeraphimBlueprint.com). Now that that modality is more secure, I am ready to return to this major endeavor.

If by the time you read this I may have organized workshops called something like "Soul Assistance," then they will be listed on my website RuthRendely.com, or perhaps on this book's website: YourMultipleSouls.com.

I wish that all your souls remain happy and healthy, today, tomorrow and forever.

Ruth Rendely

Blue Ridge Mountains

About the Author

Ruth Rendely has been a university history lecturer in America and Japan. She received her master's degree in East Asian history, as a grantee of the East-West Center, at the University of Hawaii. She then completed doctoral studies in American intellectual history at the University of Iowa. Since 1994, she began reviving an ancient angelic healing modality, known as Seraphim Blueprint, and her book *Seraphim Blueprint: The Power of Angel Healing* is available in German, Japanese, Turkish and English. She resides with her husband in the Blue Ridge Mountains of Appalachia.